TOWARDS SAFE MEDICINES

A guide to the
control of safety,
quality and efficacy
of human medicines
in the United Kingdom

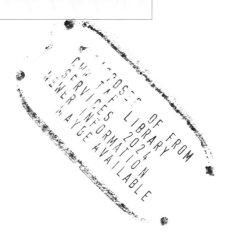

London : HMSO

Applications for reproduction should be made to HMSO

First published 1993

ISBN 0 11 321659 9

CONTENTS

PART FOUR - The UK Medicines Control Agency

PART FIVE

PART SIX

FOREWORD

The availability of medicines in the United Kingdom is controlled on the basis of their safety, quality and efficacy. This control is effected by Government in accordance with the Medicines Act of 1968 and appropriate European Community Directives issued by the Community since 1965.

Recent Government health initiatives have lent increasing encouragement to the practice of self help in the area of health care. Information on the control of medicines, however, has not been readily available in a compact, easily-readable form. This book is an attempt to remedy this deficiency and to respond in line with the aims of the Citizen's Charter, which encourages the provision of information about how public services function in language that fosters communication and openness.

It has been written to provide information which will be of interest and use to professionals, to consumer bodies, and to interested members of the public who wish to know how the development, sale and supply of human medicines in the United Kingdom is controlled.

Most medicines in general use today are the products of modern science and technology. If used wisely and properly, they can provide enormous benefits, though their use is not without inherent risk. Risk may be a consequence of the nature of the active constituents of the medicines, the possibility for human error of those in the health care professions who handle and administer these potent materials, or even accidental or incorrect use by patients.

The control of medicines has changed considerably since the implementation of the Medicines Act in September 1971. This book summarises some of the key steps taken by Government in the development of policy and in the execution of control in the manufacture and supply of medicines. Over the next few years further important changes to licensing procedures will take place as new European Community systems for the licensing of medicines come into operation. The basic concept, however, will not change, neither will the commitment on the part of the Department of Health's Medicines Control Agency to ensure that medicines available on the UK market are of the highest standards in terms of safety, efficacy and quality.

Dr K H Jones
Director and Chief Executive
UK Medicines Control Agency
London, October 1993.
An annual report with accounts is available from the Information Centre of the Medicines Control Agency.

HISTORY AND BACKGROUND

The control of medicines by officials was practiced during the reign of King Henry VIII, of England (1491-1547). It was during his reign that the Royal College of Physicians of London was empowered to appoint four fellows of the College as inspectors of apothecaries' wares in the London area, with power to destroy defective stock. In the early seventeenth century these inspecting physicians were joined by representative members of the Society of Apothecaries.

In Scotland the Charter for the Faculty of Physicians and Surgeons in Glasgow, granted in 1599 by King James VI of Scotland, also provided power to inspect and control the drugs sold in that region. The first inspector was one called William Spang.

State control of medicines according to Penn [1], however, goes back 1000 years BC to the times of the early Greeks and Egyptians. Later, in medieval times in Muslim countries, controls were exercised by the mutsahib over manufacturers of syrups who made medicinal products. Quality was regarded as important and unannounced inspections of premises led to tests to detect adulteration of raw materials. Penn also mentions the standard of quality control applied to imported spices and drugs by the Guild of Pepperers in London early in the fourteenth century. The mixing of materials of different price and quality and adulteration of any material was forbidden.

From the middle ages onwards a new concept in the control of the quality of materials for medicinal use was the preparation and publication of approved lists of drugs and authoritative information on how they should be prepared and used. These lists were the beginnings of what are now known as pharmacopoeias. The first London Pharmacopoeia was issued in 1618 followed by a second edition in 1650 and further editions till 1851. The first Edinburgh Pharmacopoeia was published in 1699 and the first Dublin Pharmacopoeia in 1807.

In 1864 the first edition of the British Pharmacopoeia was published - in effect one of the first attempts at harmonisation of standards. In the Preface, the editors described the difficulties thus:

> ... the Committees in London, Edinburgh and Dublin who had to execute the difficult task, which had previously been attempted in vain, of reducing to one standard the processes and descriptions of three different pharmacopoeias, and, what was still more difficult, of reconciling the

various usages in pharmacy and prescriptions of the peoples of three countries hitherto in these respects separate and independent.

Also during the nineteenth century the Pharmaceutical Society of Great Britain was established and legislation was introduced to control the retail sale of poisons and the people who could do this. As the nineteenth century progressed the character of medicinal products changed from materials that were mainly of plant origin to those of a synthetic chemical nature such as aspirin and the barbiturates.

The first products in the UK to be brought under a more modern control system were the biological products for which chemical tests of purity were not adequate. The 1925 Therapeutic Substances Act introduced this control. It applied to vaccines, sera, toxins, antitoxins, antigens, arsphenamines, insulin, pituitary hormone and surgical sutures. Arsphenamines were included because Salvarsan, although synthetic, contained highly toxic arsphenamine impurities which could be detected only by means of biological testing. Each batch had to be tested before release.

The Act provided for a form of licensing, which included inspection of manufacturing sites, personnel suitability and record keeping. Labelling requirements were introduced to identify the manufacturer and each batch of material produced.

Today approval for the release of material is given by an independent laboratory, the National Institute of Biological Standards and Control (NIBSC), which is a multidisciplinary establishment of international scientific reputation. It was set up in 1972.

Soon after the introduction of the National Health Service in the UK in 1948 a committee was set up to consider the practicality and desirability of limiting or prohibiting the prescribing of certain medicines. This Committee on Classification of Proprietary Medicinal Products, more often known as the *Cohen Committee* after its first chairman, the late Lord Cohen of Birkenhead, concerned itself with medicines that were already on the market. The classification of a medicine as *not of proven therapeutic value* was the most severe sanction available to this committee. Neither this committee, nor any other body, had the power to prevent the marketing of a new medicinal product.

The need for further co-ordinated legislation to cover all medicinal products was under discussion in the early 1960s, when the tragedy occurred of the births of deformed babies following the administration of thalidomide to pregnant women for the treatment of morning sickness. In a parliamentary debate on May 8 1964, Kenneth Robinson, then Minister of Health said:

> *I come to my last main topic which is the control and safety of drugs. This is of course a subject which was thrust to the fore both in this House and in the public press a year or so ago as a result of the thalidomide tragedy. The House and the public suddenly woke up to the fact that any drug manufacturer could market any product, however inadequately tested, however dangerous, without having to satisfy any independent body as to its efficacy and safety and the public was almost uniquely unprotected in this respect.*

A joint subcommittee of the Scottish and English Standing Medical Advisory Committees chaired by Lord Cohen recommended sweeping changes in legislation to control medicines. While these were being pursued in parliament the immediate setting up, in June 1963, of the Committee on Safety of Drugs (CSD) took control of new medicines a step nearer. The CSD was chaired first by the late Sir Derrick Dunlop and then by Professor Sir Eric Scowen, who also presided over the first meeting of the Committee on Safety of Medicines (CSM) in 1971. The CSD consisted of a group of independent experts in the fields of Medicine, Pharmacy, Toxicology, Pharmacology and Statistics. The Committee had the full support and co-operation of the medical and pharmaceutical professions. The pharmaceutical industry agreed to submit data on their medicinal products to the CSD and to abide by its advice. The advice of the CSD was concerned, in the words of Sir Derrick,

> *"With reasonable safety for its intended purpose,"* he continued, *"although the safety and efficacy of medicines are often inextricably intertwined, evaluation of efficacy on its own was not the function of the CSD."* [2]

A government white paper was published in September 1967 entitled *Forthcoming legislation on the Safety, Quality and Description of Drugs and Medicines.* Based on the proposals in this paper the Medicines Act was given the Royal Assent in October 1968. It became operative on 1 September 1971, the *first appointed day.* The membership of the CSD became the core of the new CSM set up under the Medicines Act.

The new Act brought most previous legislation on medicines together and also introduced a number of other legal provisions for the control of medicines. It was an enabling Act providing for a comprehensive system of licensing affecting manufacture, sale, supply and importation of medicinal products into the UK. It became unlawful to engage in these activities except in accordance with appropriate licences, certificates or exemptions.

For a period following the first appointed day, transitional exemptions enabled those engaged in the manufacture and distribution of medicinal products before licensing began, to continue with their activities. Most exemptions terminated one year later on 1 September 1972 by which time licences *as of right* had to be applied for. This licensing *as of right* was a registration exercise to provide the Licensing Authority (LA) with the information necessary for the fuller implementation of the Medicines Act. Medicinal products on the market under a product licence of right were reviewed by the Committee on the Review of Medicines (CRM) which commenced its activity in October 1975 and completed it in May 1991.

The UK was not the only country to control medicines in this fashion. Indeed, medicines control was an early area of activity of the European Economic Community (EEC). The first and basic EEC Directive to control medicines was introduced in 1965 (Directive 65/65/EEC).

The UK joined the EEC in 1973. Requirements for the control of medicinal products by the Medicines Act matched those of existing European Directives and in some instances went beyond them (for example for Clinical Trials). During the ensuing years the UK contributed, together with other member states, to the development and updating of the EEC Directives in this area. European Community (EC) legislation now takes precedence over the Medicines Act, its Instruments and Orders (subordinate legislation), which are amended from time to time to align with new EC requirements.

Safety, quality and efficacy are the only criteria on which legislation to control human medicines is founded, within the United Kingdom and within the EC.

[1] Penn, R.G. The State Control of Medicines: The First 3000 Years. *British Journal of Clinical Pharmacology*. 1979, 8, 293-305.

[2] Dunlop, D. Medicines in our Time. *Nuffield Provincial Hospital Trust*, 1973.

LIST OF ABBREVIATIONS

ABPI	Association of British Pharmaceutical Industry
ADROIT	Adverse Drug Reaction On-line Information Tracking
BAN	British Approved Name
BP	British Pharmacopoeia
BMA	British Medical Association
BPC	British Pharmacopoeia Commission
BNF	British National Formulary
CDSM	Committee on Dental and Surgical Materials
CIOMS	Council for International Organisations of Medical Science
CPMP	Committee for Proprietary Medicinal Products
CRM	Committee on the Review of Medicines
CSD	Committee on Safety of Drugs
CSM	Committee on Safety of Medicines
CTC	Clinical Trial Certificate
CTX	Clinical Trial Exemption
CVMP	Committee for Veterinary Medicinal Products
DG	Directorates General
DMRC	Defective Medicines Report Centre
DH	Department of Health
DNA	Deoxyribonucleic Acid
DTI	Department of Trade and Industry
EEC	European Economic Community
EC	European Community
EMEA	European Medicines Evaluation Agency
GMP	Good Manufacturing Practice
GSL	General Sale List Medicine
HMSO	Her Majesty's Stationery Office
IAG	Inspection Action Group
IT	Information Technology
ITC	Independent Television Companies
LA	Licensing Authority
MA	Marketing Authorisation
MAFF	Ministry of Agriculture Fisheries and Food
MAIL	Medicines Act Information Letter
MC	Medicines Commission
MCA	Medicines Control Agency
MDD	Medical Devices Directorate

ML	Manufacturer's Licence
NAS	New Active Substance
NIBSC	National Institute of Biological Standards and Control
NPF	Nurse Prescribers' Formulary
OTC	Over-the-Counter
P	Pharmacy only Medicine
PAGB	Proprietary Association of Great Britain
PER	Product Evaluation Report
Ph Eur	Pharmacopée Européenne
PIC	Pharmaceutical Inspection Convention
PIL	Product Information Leaflet
PL(PI)	Product Licence (Parallel Import)
PL	Product Licence
PLR	Product Licence of Right
POM	Prescription Only Medicine
PQ	Parliamentary Question
RCP	Royal College of Physicians
RCGP	Royal College of General Practitioners
RPSGB	Royal Pharmaceutical Society of Great Britain
S4	Section 4 (Medicines Act) Committee
SI	Statutory Instrument
SPC	Summary of Product Characteristics
TSA	Therapeutic Substances Act
USP	United States Pharmacopoeia
WDL	Wholesale Dealer's Licence
WHO	World Health Organisation

PART ONE

Medicines and
the Licensing Authority

Some essential facts

WHAT IS A MEDICINE?

The Medicines Act 1968 defines a medicinal product as a substance or article intended for use mainly or wholly for a medicinal purpose. A medicinal purpose is defined as finding out the existence, degree or extent of a physiological condition; diagnosing, preventing or treating disease; inducing anaesthesia; or otherwise preventing or interfering with the normal operation of a physiological function, which includes, for example, contraception.

Within the meaning of this Act the term *medicinal product* does not include such things as instruments, appliances or devices, for example, heart pacemakers. However, some biological, surgical, dental and ophthalmic materials are specified in the Medicines Act or its subordinate legislation. Examples of specified medicinal products are intra-uterine devices and contact lens fluids.

Medicines come in a variety of pharmaceutical forms depending on the condition to be treated and the way in which this may be done. For example, solid dosage forms such as lozenges, pastilles, tablets, pills and capsules can be designed to dissolve slowly in the mouth; or more rapidly in the stomach for better absorption or to pass through the stomach to dissolve lower in the gut; or to give a controlled release of medicament throughout the gut.

External forms of medication include lotions, creams, ointments, liniments and skin patches. Aerosols can provide medication topically to the lungs for the rapid relief of asthma; suitable drops can carry medicaments to the eyes, ears and nose. Specially designed solid dose forms such as pessaries and suppositories carry medication into the vagina and rectum. Injections may be used to introduce medication through the skin into blood vessels or to subcutaneous tissues, muscles and other tissues in the body.

The purpose of these various forms of medication is to carry the active constituent (the drug) to the area where it is most needed and in so doing to avoid, or keep to a minimum, any unwanted effects on other areas of the body.

BORDERLINE PRODUCTS

Although most human medicines are clearly identifiable as such, and subject to licensing, there are borderline cases.

A substance which is for use solely as a toilet preparation (see below), food, beverage, or disinfectant is not within the scope of the Medicines Act.

A dietary supplement containing such familiar substances as vitamins, amino acids, or minerals is not subject to medicines control unless medicinal claims are made for it. It is, however, subject to food laws.

A toilet preparation or cosmetic is a substance or preparation intended to be applied to the various surfaces of the human body wholly or mainly for a variety of purposes such as perfuming, cleansing, protecting, caring or keeping in good condition, combating body odours or normal body perspiration. These are subject to cosmetic laws. However, even if the product complies with the above, it is not exempt if written claims are made for remedial or curative functions in connection with human disease. Claims are considered in the context of the product, its constituents and how it is presented.

There are special cases where exemptions do not apply and these are when an antibiotic is included in the formula, or when more than 0.004% (by weight) of a hormone, or more than 1.0% (by weight) of resorcinol are present. If a cosmetic product is promoted to the medical or dental professions for a medicinal purpose it is not exempt from the provisions of the Medicines Act.

Bandages and other surgical dressings are not subject to the provisions of the Act except where they are medicated and the medication has a curative function. In many cases, for example hair restorers, anti-smoking preparations, alcoholic beverages, the nature of the claims made or indications given on the labels or promotional material may be crucial in deciding whether the purpose of administration is wholly or mainly medicinal.

The Medicines Control Agency (MCA) will advise applicants, manufacturers, or other interested parties in cases of doubt.

The flow chart in figure 1 outlines the process of determining the status of medicinal products for human use.

FIGURE 1

DETERMINATION OF STATUS OF PRODUCTS FOR HUMAN USE

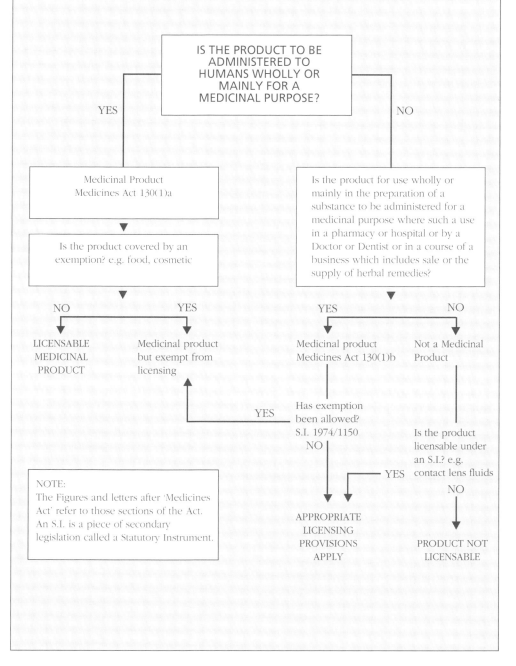

IS THE PRODUCT TO BE ADMINISTERED TO HUMANS WHOLLY OR MAINLY FOR A MEDICINAL PURPOSE?

YES

NO

Medicinal Product
Medicines Act 130(1)a

Is the product for use wholly or mainly in the preparation of a substance to be administered for a medicinal purpose where such a use in a pharmacy or hospital or by a Doctor or Dentist or in a course of a business which includes sale or the supply of herbal remedies?

Is the product covered by an exemption? e.g. food, cosmetic

NO   YES   YES   NO

LICENSABLE
MEDICINAL
PRODUCT

Medicinal product
but exempt from
licensing

Medicinal product
Medicines Act 130(1)b

Not a Medicinal
Product

YES

Has exemption
been allowed?
S.I. 1974/1150
NO

Is the product
licensable under
an S.I.? e.g.
contact lens fluids

YES

NO

NOTE:
The Figures and letters after 'Medicines Act' refer to those sections of the Act. An S.I. is a piece of secondary legislation called a Statutory Instrument.

APPROPRIATE
LICENSING
PROVISIONS
APPLY

PRODUCT NOT
LICENSABLE

CLASSIFICATION OF MEDICINAL PRODUCTS

The Medicines Act divides medicines for human use into three categories for the purpose of retail sale or supply: General Sale List (GSL), Pharmacy (P) and Prescription Only Medicine (POM).

- **General Sale List.** The purpose of this list is to specify those medicinal products which can be sold with reasonable safety without the supervision of a pharmacist, for example in a supermarket.

- **Pharmacy.** Pharmacy medicines do not require a prescription and may be sold or supplied only in a registered pharmacy by or under the supervision of a pharmacist. The package gives information on dosage.

- **Prescription Only Medicine.** These medicines may be sold or supplied only from a registered pharmacy and in accordance with a prescription issued by a doctor or dentist. The substances so restricted are those whose use needs to be supervised by a medical or dental practitioner because the condition being treated requires diagnosis by a doctor or dentist and because they may produce toxic reaction or physical or psychological dependence, or may be a hazard to the health of the community. The criteria for these restrictions are set out in the Medicines Act.

The general rule is that all licensed medicines are P unless otherwise designated. Substances are listed in the GSL and POM orders on the advice of committees set up by the Medicines Commission. These lists are available to the public and they are revised periodically when new medicines come on the market.

New active substances (NAS) (see Part Four, New Drugs Business, for explanation) contained in newly licensed medicinal products may be made POM temporarily through the licence and will be added to the POM list if permanent prescription control is needed. For licence applications containing established ingredients, legal status is automatically determined by the existing POM and GSL orders which specify the category, POM, P or GSL, to which the medicines should belong. To alter the legal status of any substance generally requires an amendment of the relevant order. The procedure involves widespread consultations with appropriate bodies and organisations outside the MCA.

THE LICENSING AUTHORITY AND ITS ACCOUNTABILITY

The Licensing Authority (LA) for human medicines in the UK consists of Government Ministers comprising the Minister of Health, the Minister of Agriculture Fisheries and Food and Ministers in government health departments in Scotland and Northern Ireland.

The Secretary of State for Health, acting on behalf of the other Ministers comprising the LA is responsible for the control of medicines for human use in the UK. The United Kingdom Medicines Control Agency (MCA) is the executive arm of Government which regulates the pharmaceutical sector and implements policy in this area (see Part Four). Its constitution and responsibilities are defined in a publicly-available document called the Framework Document. The MCA is led by a Chief Executive who reports to the Secretary of State.

In accordance with the requirements of the Framework Document establishing the MCA, an Annual Report with Accounts is published. An annual meeting is also held at which the MCA makes a public statement of its performance and its proposals for future activity. This is attended by a wide range of delegates, including representatives from the pharmaceutical industry, professional bodies and consumer organisations.

The MCA's primary objective is to safeguard public health by ensuring that all medicines on the UK market meet appropriate standards of safety, quality and efficacy. *Safety* aspects encompass potential or actual harmful effects; *quality* aspects relate to development and manufacture; and *efficacy* deals with the beneficial effect of the medicine on the patient, in other words *does it work?*. The safeguarding of public health is achieved largely through a system of licensing and subsequent monitoring of medicines after they have been licensed. The MCA also has an Inspectorate which is responsible for supervising and enforcing standards of pharmaceutical manufacture and wholesaling. Pharmacopoeial standards for the quality of materials used in medicinal products are provided by means of the British and European pharmacopoeias (see section 6 for more details).

Medical, pharmaceutical and scientific staff of the MCA, working in multi-disciplinary functional teams, assess the scientific data supplied by an applicant for a product licence (*or marketing authorisation* to use EC terminology).

Applications derive mainly from the pharmaceutical industry but anyone with the necessary supporting data may apply for a licence. The task of evaluating the risk/benefit ratio (evaluation of the beneficial effects of the medicine against the possible harmful effects) of any medicine is complex. Evaluation takes into account the nature of the active constituents, the dosage form (for example tablet or liquid), the nature of the disease or condition to be treated, the effective dose that needs to be given, the type of patient (for example, age) and the duration of treatment. A high risk-to-benefit ratio may be acceptable in the treatment of terminally-ill patients where the quality of life might be enhanced, whereas a very low risk-to-benefit ratio is expected in the treatment of patients with self-limiting diseases, for the purpose of prophylaxis (eg vaccines) and for those requiring life-long treatment for their illnesses.

In arriving at a decision whether or not to grant a licence, the LA frequently takes independent expert advice on matters relating to safety, quality and efficacy from advisory bodies. These advisory bodies are the Medicines Commission and Committees appointed under Section 4 (S4) of the Medicines Act, such as the Committee on Safety of Medicines (CSM) and the Committee on Dental and Surgical Materials (CDSM). Expert sub-committees on safety, quality and efficacy serve these committees.

These bodies consist of independent experts who are appointed by Ministers. They do not include members of staff of the MCA. MCA staff, however, provide to these bodies for their consideration critical evaluations of the pharmaceutical, medical and scientific data supplied by applicants for product licences. Secretariat support to the advisory bodies is also provided by MCA staff.

ADVISORY BODIES SET UP UNDER THE MEDICINES ACT

The Medicines Commission is the statutory advisory body specified in the Medicines Act and has a broadly-based membership. The Commission provides advice to the LA on all matters relating to the implementation of the Medicines Act and on medicines in general. It hears appeals by applicants for product licences against proposed adverse LA decisions (see figure 2).

The members of the Commission are appointed by Ministers after wide consultation with such organisations as they consider appropriate in relation to activities in the practice of medicine, veterinary medicine, pharmacy, chemistry (other than pharmaceutical chemistry) and the pharmaceutical industry. Wide and recent experience with acknowledged capacity in a particular activity is required of members.

Committees set up under the recommendation of the Medicines Commission include:

*   **Committee on Safety of Medicines (CSM).** This committee advises the LA on questions of the safety, quality and efficacy of new medicines for human use. It is also responsible for *encouraging* the collection and investigation of reports on suspected adverse reactions to medicines already on the market. A number of specialist sub-committees have been established to assist the committee in its work.

*   **Committee on Dental and Surgical Materials (CDSM).** This committee, as its name implies, has a function identical to that of the CSM providing advice on a range of specialist products which fall outside the expertise of the CSM.

The work of a further committee, established under Section 4 of the Medicines Act, the **Committee on the Review of Medicines (CRM),** was completed in the Spring of 1991. It advised the LA on the review of the safety, quality and efficacy of those products, with certain exceptions, eg homoeopathics, that had been on the market prior to the Medicines Act taking effect and had been granted product licences of right.

FIGURE 2

THE MEDICINES COMMISSION

Advises Ministers on policy on medicines and the Medicine Act

•

Hears appeals on product licences and trial certificates

•

Advises Ministers on scope and membership of
Medicines Act Committees

•

Recommends to Ministers publication of works including new
editions of the British Pharmacopoeia

| The 1968 Medicines Act set up the Medicines Commission which in turn advised on the setting up of specialist Committees | The Committees give advice to the licensing authority on applications for product licences and on proposals to suspend, revoke or vary licences | The Commission considers appeals from applicants against the Committees' advice and gives its own advice to the licensing authority | The licensing authority decides whether to grant, revoke, suspend or vary a product licence |

THE BRITISH PHARMACOPOEIA COMMISSION

Another body set up under Section 4 of the Medicines Act is the British Pharmacopoeia Commission (BPC) which is the national pharmacopoeial authority of the UK.

Pharmacopoeial standards are standards of quality for materials used in medicinal products and are provided by means of the British and European Pharmacopoeias (BP and Ph Eur - Pharmacopée Européenne).

The Pharmacopoeia is an important statutory component of the overall system of the control of medicines and complements the licensing and inspection processes of the MCA. Pharmacopoeial standards are published and readily available to all who need to use them - suppliers, purchasers, medicines regulators or independent laboratories. They provide the manufacturing industry with a clear yardstick of quality for many commonly used medicines and their ingredients. Pharmacopoeial standards contribute to an assurance of the identity and purity of these medicines and their constituents throughout their shelf-life.

The BPC and its secretariat (MCA staff) are responsible for the preparation of the BP publication and for UK participation in the preparation of the Ph Eur. The Ph Eur specifications are incorporated into the BP so that all official published UK standards for medicines for human use are available in a single compendium. Provision of publicly available specifications calls for a broad range of expertise and the BPC and its subsidiary committees include members from academia, hospitals, relevant industries and professional bodies. The European Pharmacopoeia Commission, set up under the Council of Europe, is composed of delegations from countries who are members of the Council of Europe together with its groups of experts, and has a similarly broadly-based membership.

The BPC and its secretariat are also responsible for devising British Approved Names (BAN's) which are shortened versions of often long and complicated chemical and biotechnological names for newly-discovered active substances.

COMMUNICATION WITH OTHER BODIES

As well as consultation with the advisory bodies on matters of licensing, the MCA is in regular contact with other interested parties.

The European Commission is having an increasing influence on the work of the MCA. The Commission's Directorates-General propose new legislation in the form of Regulations and Directives for the control of medicinal products. This is an on-going task, which takes account of increasing knowledge and experience (see Section 12 for fuller information).

In the UK there is constant interaction between the MCA, the public and politicians by means of Parliamentary Questions (PQ's) and direct correspondence. The number of PQ's concerned with the control of human medicines is about 100 per year.

Medical and allied professions are made aware of current drug safety problems through a bulletin entitled *Current Problems*.

Licence holders regularly receive a copy of the Medicines Act Information Letter (MAIL). These letters deal with issues such as EC Directives and Guidelines; licensing procedure amendments; changes in MCA staff responsibilities; changes in fees; assessment times for licensing applications; pharmacopoeial matters; and veterinary matters.

Trade associations have regular meetings with the MCA to discuss matters of mutual interest and how problems can be solved without jeopardising the health of the patient.

Other sections of Government such as the Department of Trade and Industry (DTI), the Home Office, the Ministry of Agriculture, Fisheries and Food (MAFF) and the Medical Devices Directorate (MDD) are advised and consulted as necessary on matters affecting their interests.

MCA staff represent and deal with UK interests in relation to certain World Health Organisation (WHO) activities. Delegations from overseas Governments are received as guests of the MCA to discuss matters of medicines control in this and their own countries.

The relationship between the MCA, its advisory bodies and others is illustrated in figure 3.

FIGURE 3

MCA INTERACTION
WITH OTHER ORGANISATIONS

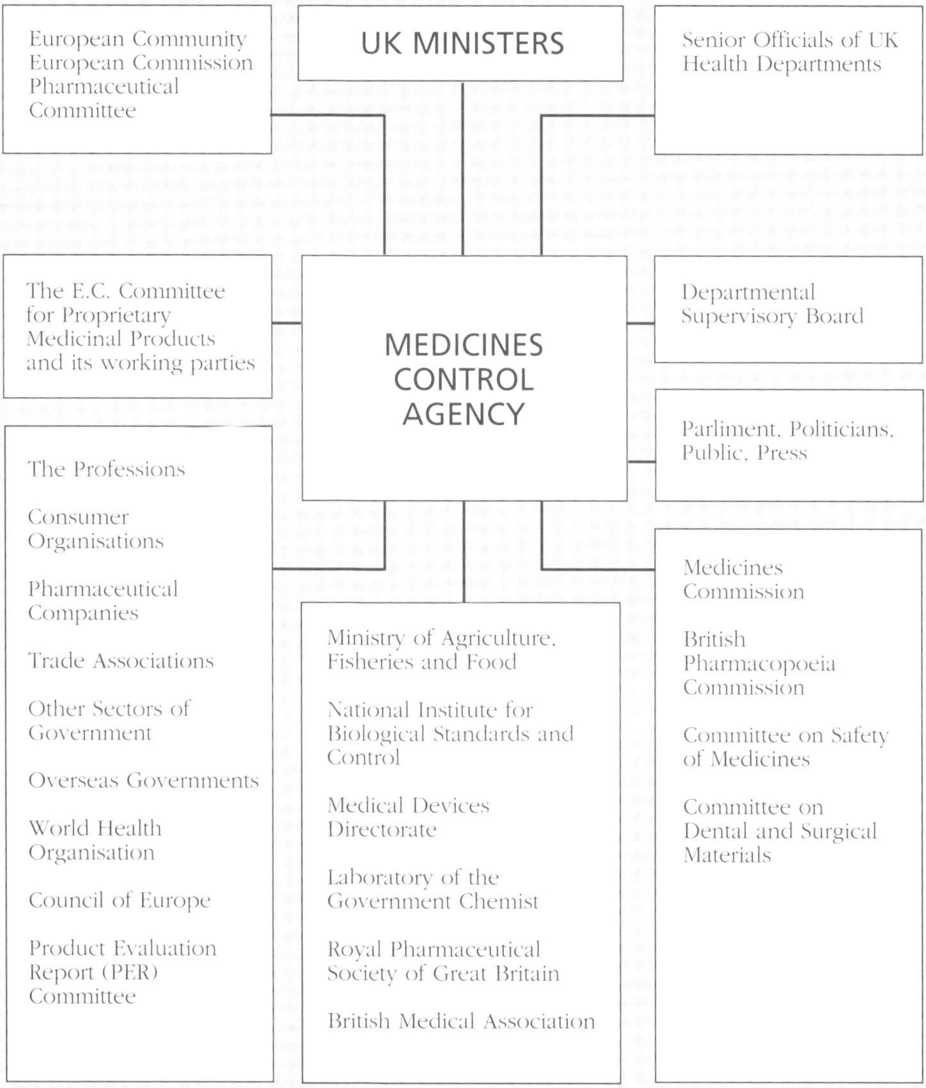

European Community
European Commission
Pharmaceutical
Committee

UK MINISTERS

Senior Officials of UK
Health Departments

The E.C. Committee
for Proprietary
Medicinal Products
and its working parties

MEDICINES
CONTROL
AGENCY

Departmental
Supervisory Board

Parliment, Politicians,
Public, Press

The Professions

Consumer
Organisations

Pharmaceutical
Companies

Trade Associations

Other Sectors of
Government

Overseas Governments

World Health
Organisation

Council of Europe

Product Evaluation
Report (PER)
Committee

Ministry of Agriculture,
Fisheries and Food

National Institute for
Biological Standards and
Control

Medical Devices
Directorate

Laboratory of the
Government Chemist

Royal Pharmaceutical
Society of Great Britain

British Medical Association

Medicines
Commission

British
Pharmacopoeia
Commission

Committee on Safety
of Medicines

Committee on
Dental and Surgical
Materials

PART TWO

The Licensing System

TYPES OF LICENCES/CERTIFICATES GRANTED BY THE LICENSING AUTHORITY

The main types of licences and certificates granted by the LA are product licences (PL), parallel imports (PLPI), clinical trial certificates (CTC), manufacturer's licences (ML), and wholesale dealer's licences (WDL). The LA also administers a clinical trial exemption scheme (CTX).

- **Product Licence (PL)**

A product licence authorises the holder to sell, supply or export the medicinal product in question; procure the sale, supply or export of the product; procure the manufacture or assembly (that is packaging and labelling) of the product for sale, supply, or export; or import the product.

The product licence thus covers all the main activities associated with the marketing of a medicinal product. The product licence holder is the person *responsible for the composition* of the product who is either the person to whose order the product is manufactured or, in any other case, the manufacturer.

Applications for product licences are made to the LA. They must be accompanied by relevant supporting data relating to pharmaceutical quality, safety and clinical efficacy in the proposed indications. Detailed guidelines based on European Directives on quality, pre-clinical testing and clinical trial requirements, are issued by the LA which must satisfy itself regarding the quality, safety and efficacy of the product before granting a licence. The need for the product, its price and its efficacy compared to existing products, are not relevant issues for consideration by the LA under the terms of the Medicines Act. When an application first arrives at the MCA it undergoes examination by MCA staff to determine its compliance with requirements and suitability for consideration within the terms of licensing procedures. If the LA wishes to refuse an application it must first consult the appropriate advisory committee, that is the CSM or the CDSM. The applicant has the right to make representations against a negative decision in writing, or orally *(a hearing)*, to the appropriate committee if the LA intends to refuse the application. The applicant also has the right to make further representations to the Medicines Commission if the LA still intends to refuse the application after considering the representations before the appropriate committee. The applicant may also make representations before a person appointed by the LA in certain circumstances. In all cases, the various advisory bodies may only provide advice. The LA is the only body with the power to grant or withhold licences although the advice of the advisory committees is always weighed very carefully before a decision is made.

Approximately 90% of all licence applications are dealt with by the Licensing Authority without reference to Advisory bodies. In practice applications are assessed initially by MCA staff who may wish to ask for clarification of doubtful points or for more information to substantiate statements made in the application. The authority to do this is contained in Section 44 of the Medicines Act. MCA staff may, therefore, contact the applicant and request any additional information under this section of the Act.

It is current practice for licence applications for all medicines containing new active substances to be referred for comment and advice to the advisory bodies. Most abridged applications (see Part Four, Abridged Licensing Business, for explanation) and requests for variations to existing licences are dealt with in-house by MCA staff alone. Some abridged cases are, however, referred to the advisory bodies where it is considered that special problems might exist. Such applications may include those requesting a new route of synthesis of an active drug substance; a novel dose delivery system, for example a new controlled release mechanism; an extension of clinical indications; or a significant change in dosage regimen.

As indicated above, the advisory bodies, with the support of their specialist sub-committees who carry out a detailed consideration of issues relevant to them, may decide to recommend to the LA that an application be refused or granted subject to certain changes being made in the application. Before the LA takes action the applicant is advised by the advisory body's secretariat, under the authority of Section 21 of the Act, of the advisory body's advice.

- **Product Licence (Parallel Import) (PLPI)**

Parallel importing involves buying medicines in one EC member state and selling them in another, at a profit. The granting of licences in the EC for such a purpose began in 1984. The conditions for granting a parallel import licence in a member state, for example the UK, is that the product must be licensed in an EC member state; have no difference in therapeutic effect from a product licensed in the UK; be manufactured by the same group of companies, or by another company under licence, as the UK product and be labelled in English, although additional languages are not prohibited.

• Clinical Trial Certificate (CTC)

A clinical trial is an investigation by a doctor or dentist involving administration of a medicinal product to a patient to assess the product's safety and efficacy. Applications for clinical trial certificates are made to the LA in the same way as applications for product licences. Supporting data on quality and relevant safety are required and detailed guidelines on the data requirements are issued by the LA. Applications are assessed in the same way as product licence applications. Efficacy is not an issue in determining applications for clinical trial certificates because clinical trials are usually conducted to determine whether or not a new medicine is efficacious. The same legal rights regarding representations to advisory committees and the Medicines Commission apply to these applications as to product licences.

During the first ten years of the control of medicines in the UK all new active substances, and some established substances for new clinical indications, were evaluated in patients under a clinical trial certificate. Most trials are now conducted under an exemption scheme.

This exemption scheme for clinical trials (see next section) was introduced in 1981 to speed up the trial of new substances. More than 90% of all clinical trials are now carried out under this scheme. If a medicinal product on a market outside the UK is imported for a clinical trial it must be authorised for this purpose by a certificate or exemption which expressly refers to the trial.

A manufacturer's licence is not required for the manufacture or assembly of a medicinal product for the sole purpose of a clinical trial.

• Clinical Trial Exemption Scheme (CTX)

Since 1981 pharmaceutical manufacturers and suppliers may supply medicinal products for the purpose of conducting clinical trials without holding clinical trial certificates or product licences under the provisions of this scheme. The main requirements for this exemption are that the supplier notifies the LA of his intention to supply investigators (doctors or dentists who are going to conduct the clinical trial) and supports this with a summary of the relevant pharmaceutical data (information on the manufacture and composition of the product) and the pre-clinical safety data (information on the testing of the product in animals).

The Clinical Trial Exemption Scheme is computer based and all summary data are recorded on disc. This enables sophisticated assessment and control of all trials to be made by experienced professional assessors within statutory time constraints (normally 35 days but this may be extended by another 28 days to give the LA more time to process a complex application). There are, therefore, minimal delays in allowing important new medicinal products to be evaluated in patients.

Other conditions associated with this exemption scheme are that:

- a registered medical practitioner must certify the accuracy of the summary;

- the supplier undertakes to inform the LA of any refusal to permit the trial by an ethics committee;

- the supplier also undertakes to inform the LA of any data or reports which affect the safety of the product.

There are no rights of appeal against a refusal to grant a CTX.

- **Licensing Process**

Figure 4 illustrates the process of licensing.

- *Validation:* an application is considered to be legally valid for passage through the licensing system when it complies with the requirements in the *EC Notice to Applicants* for administrative and scientific data.

- *44* refers to a section in the Medicines Act whereby the LA may request additional information.

- *21(1)* and *21(3)* refer to sections in the Medicines Act concerning a S4 committee's intention to recommend refusal of an application.

FIGURE 4

STAGES IN THE PROGRESS OF AN APPLICATION THROUGH THE LICENSING SYSTEM

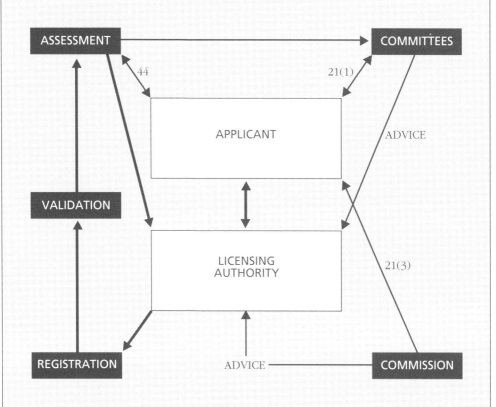

Stages in the progress of an application through the UK licensing system

The process is primarily one of communication between an applicant and the Licensing Authority. The Advisory Bodies, such as the Committee on Safety of Medicines set up under section 4 of the Medicines Act, are there to give the Licensing Authority advice in making its decisions.

- Applications are made by an applicant, mainly from the Pharmaceutical Industry, to the Licensing Authority (LA) for Clinical Trial Certificates (CTC), Clinical Trial Exemptions (CTX), Product Licences (PL - equivalent to EC Marketing Authorisation, MA), Parallel Import Product Licenses (PLPI), and variations to and renewal of the above.

- The LA registers the application and validates it, i.e. checks that all necessary data and reports required by the EC Notice to Applicants are present.

- Assessors from the New Drugs Business deal with New Active Substances (NAS), CTC, CTX, Biological Products and applications for the CPMP systems. All other applications are dealt with by the Abridged Licensing Business.

- Assessors may request, under section 44 of the Medicines Act, further information or clarification of data submitted.

- Assessors may also request advice from a Section 4 Committee.

- If a Section 4 Committee is minded to advise the LA to refuse an application (Section 21(1) of the Act) the applicant has the right of a hearing (either written or oral) before the Committee. If, after the hearing, the Committee is still minded to advise against the granting of a licence the applicant has the right to appeal to the Medicines Commission (Section 21(3) of the Act). Such an appeal can be on scientific and technical matters only.

- Assessors determine the application taking account of expert advice, where sought, by reference to its safety, quality, and efficacy.

- Licences, certificates, variations and renewals are then prepared by the Abridged Licensing Businesses and issued to the Applicant.

• Manufacturer's Licence (ML)

Manufacture includes any process carried out in the course of making a medicinal product. A manufacturer's licence is also needed to cover assembly, for example, filling or labelling the final container for the product. There are nearly 500 manufacturing sites in the UK, each of which is inspected by the MCA Inspectorate at least every two years. The EC principles of good manufacturing practice (GMP) are the basis for the standards applied to the making of medicinal products. Quality cannot be established by testing a sample of a product alone but must be built into the product at all stages of production. GMP, therefore, is essential to giving an assurance of quality. The EC guide to GMP is particularly concerned with those aspects of quality, safety and efficacy which may be affected by manufacturing processes carried out on any scale and gives recommendations applicable to each process.

Quality control is that part of GMP concerned with the sampling and testing of raw materials and finished products and with the organisation, documentation and release procedures which make sure that all necessary and appropriate tests have been carried out. Quality control also includes the personnel, their selection, training, qualifications and aptitude involved in these functions.

To achieve effective control of quality, GMP requires that a manufacturer possesses the appropriate facilities with respect to premises, equipment, staff and expertise and operates an effective quality assurance system. Normally, before a licence is granted, an inspection of the premises is made and the LA has to assess these factors and take them into account before reaching a decision.

• Wholesale Dealer's Licence (WDL)

Wholesale dealing covers the sale of a product to a person who buys the product for the purpose of sale or supply to someone else; it also covers sale to a practitioner for administration to his patients. Licensing of wholesalers is concerned primarily with identification of the distributor, the suitability of the premises used for storage of products and adequate turnover of stock. There are some 1800 in the UK, most of whom tend to specialise in one or two products or in a particular section of the market. About 80 are *full-line wholesalers* providing a full range of pharmaceutical products. Wholesalers are inspected before a licence is granted and thereafter at least once during the five-year period of the licence.

PERIOD OF VALIDITY/SANCTIONS/ VARIATIONS

- ### Period of validity of licences and certificates

Licences are granted for periods up to five years and Clinical Trial Certificates for two years. They may be renewed at the end of this time by application to the LA before expiry of the current licence. On renewal they must reflect the current state of the art of manufacture, quality assurance and administration of the medicinal product. CTX's are valid for three years and can also be renewed.

- ### Sanctions

There are provisions in the Act under which the LA may vary, suspend or revoke a licence, Such action is usually taken on grounds of safety. Ordinarily, any proposed action by the LA will allow the holder the right to make representations, in writing or orally, before such action is taken. For product licences and clinical trial certificates representations are made to the appropriate advisory committee and there is a further right to make representation to the Medicines Commission if the LA still intends to take action against the licence. In the case of manufacturers' and wholesale dealers' licences representations against proposed actions by the LA are made direct to the LA since no advisory committees are involved. Representations may be made in writing or by a judicial hearing.

If it appears to the LA that, in the interests of safety, it is necessary to suspend a licence urgently, it may do so with immediate effect (without permitting the holder the right to make representations) for a period not exceeding three months in the first instance. This provision is invoked only when, in the judgement of the LA, it would not be defensible in terms of patient safety to permit the delay involved in the standard procedure.

- ### Variations to licences and certificates

When a new product is launched on to the market it is monitored closely in all aspects of its production, distribution and use. Production may begin on a small scale but if demand for the product increases the manufacturer may need to use different and, perhaps, more sophisticated equipment to meet demand. There may be a need to transfer production to a bigger factory or even to build a new factory. A decision to package it differently or introduce new pack sizes may be required. On the clinical side there may be a wish to expand the indications and alter the dosage. Changes to the Data Sheet (see Part Three, Advertising, for description) may be required. Such changes require the holder of the licence or certificate to apply to the LA to vary the licence. On average licences for new products are varied about a dozen times in the first eighteen months to two years of life.

If the LA, which may take advice from an advisory committee, does not agree with the proposed change, the holder does not have the right to make representations to an advisory committee or to the LA.   The submission of a new abridged application, (see Part Four, Abridged Licensing Business, for definition) however, instead of a variation, would confer these rights. If the LA itself proposes a variation, as previously indicated, and the licence holder objects to the proposed change, there is right in this case to make representations.

EXEMPTIONS FROM LICENSING

The Medicines Act contains certain important exemptions from licensing and makes provision for further exemptions to be included in statutory orders. The more important exemptions are outlined below.

- **Healthy volunteers**

Substances administered to human beings for experimental purposes where there is no knowledge or any evidence that the administration is likely to be beneficial and where administration is solely by way of a test for ascertaining the effects of the substance, are not *medicinal products* within the meaning of the Act. An investigation of the above nature is not therefore regarded as a clinical trial and a clinical trial certificate or exemption is not required to permit its execution. Those who volunteer for such trials are called *healthy volunteers*, a term not defined or mentioned in the Act.

Such experiments, however, are part of the normal process of drug development and contribute to progress in medical research into finding new ways of treating disease. If such studies have been performed the results are required to be included with the data submitted to the LA, in support of an application for a clinical trial certificate/exemption or for a product licence.

Control of healthy volunteer studies takes the form of regulation by the medical profession through independent ethics committees which include members other than those in the medical profession. This control follows advice to the Health Ministers by the Medicines Commission and guidelines laid down by the Royal College of Physicians (RCP) and those of the Association of British Pharmaceutical Industry (ABPI). These guidelines cover the reason for the study; the objectives of the study; the selection of healthy volunteers; the design and procedures of the study; the dosage and sampling times; clinical monitoring; measurement of various parameters; statistical methods of analysis and administrative aspects covering ethical and legal considerations.

- **Doctors and Dentists**

Treatment of particular patients A doctor or dentist is not required to hold a product licence or clinical trial certificate for a product prepared to his own prescription for administration to a particular patient. Nor is he required to hold a manufacturer's licence for this purpose, although a manufacturer who makes up a product to the order of a doctor or dentist may need to hold a manufacturer's licence to make these unlicensed *specials*.

This exemption reflects the important principle that legislation is not intended to interfere with the treatment of patients by their doctor. This exemption does not apply to other practitioners such as homoeopaths and naturopaths. Various special licences are available, however, to cover these latter activities.

Clinical trials A doctor or dentist may be supplied with a stock of a medicinal product that is not covered by a licence or a certificate for the purpose of conducting a clinical trial. The essential requirements are that the trial is undertaken on the initiative of the doctor or dentist without the instigation of the manufacturer or any third party and that the doctor or dentist is entirely responsible for the patients concerned. Request for exemption from the need to hold a certificate must be made before the trial begins. A request for exemption must include summary information about the aim of the trial and some details of the protocol and information on the trial drug proposed for use. The LA has the power to object on the ground of safety and has 21 days in which to do so.

- **Nurses and Midwives**

Registered nurses and certified midwives do not require a manufacturer's licence in order to assemble medicinal products in the course of their professional activities.

As far as prescribing licensed medicines and appliances for patients is concerned the Government supported the recommendation of the 1986 Cumberlege report on community nursing that appropriately qualified district nurses, midwives and health visitors be permitted to prescribe from an agreed nurse prescribers' formulary (NPF). In March 1992 the Medicinal Products : Prescription by Nurses etc Act 1992 became law to come into operation in October 1993. This necessitates a change in the Prescription Only Medicines Order (the POM Order).

- **Pharmacists**

In certain circumstances products may be made up without the need for the manufacturer to hold a manufacturer's licence. This exemption applies to pharmacists preparing or dispensing products in a hospital or pharmacy in accordance with a practitioner's prescription. It also applies to anyone assembling products under supervision of a registered pharmacist provided that the products, which are not to be advertised, are for sale at that pharmacy.

The pharmacist is also exempt from the need to hold licences where preparation or dispensing of non-prescription medicinal products in a registered pharmacy is done for patients requesting advice and where the pharmacist's judgement decides a suitable treatment. This is sometimes called *counter prescribing*.

However, the need for these activities is on the decline since most medicines are pre-packed in the final container and the use of *patient pack* is on the increase. The pharmacist's role in the community is changing. A Committee of Inquiry appointed by the Nuffield Foundation to consider the present and future structure of the practice of pharmacy in its several branches and its potential contribution to health care issued a report in 1986. It concluded, among other things, that pharmacists in community practice have a unique and vital role to play in the provision of health care. This conclusion was endorsed and expanded in the 1992 report of the joint working party on the future role of the community pharmaceutical services.

PRODUCTS OF LONG STANDING AND/OR NOT ORIGINALLY SUBJECT TO EC DIRECTIVES.

When the Medicines Act came into effect in 1971 provision was made for the granting of product licences of right in respect of medicinal products which were already on the market in the UK. Such licences were granted automatically without specific consideration of quality, safety or efficacy. In effect this was a registration procedure and was completed within one year of the Medicines Act being implemented. Holders of product licences of right (PLRs) were advised that review and assessment would take place later and were encouraged to prepare for this exercise.

EC Directive 75/318/EEC indicated that with certain exceptions medicines should be reviewed by May 1990. In the UK the review began in 1975, with the setting up of the CRM, and was completed for human medicines in the spring of 1991.

When the review began there were over 39,000 PLRs registered. A number of these were *specials* produced to order on a small manufacturing scale by industry for hospital pharmacies to meet local requirements. Also included in this number were some 6,000 PLRs for homoeopathic products (medicines containing extremely small amounts of active constituents and manufactured in a special way); blood products (medicines made from human blood or plasma such as Factor VIII used to control bleeding in haemophiliac patients); immunologicals (vaccines, toxins, sera and allergens); and radiopharmaceuticals (medicines containing a radioactive component and used mainly for diagnostic or testing purposes). These were excluded by EC Directive from the 1990 deadline. However, in the UK vaccines and immunologicals were included in the early review and blood products and radiopharmaceuticals followed later.

The review began by considering therapeutic categories such as analgesics, non-steroid anti-inflammatory drugs and psychotropic medicines. Frequency of reported suspected adverse drug reactions contributed to giving these categories priority. In considering these products the quality of the active constituents, the appropriate dose for maximum therapeutic effect, the need for warnings, and adverse effects to be included in data sheets, labelling and advertising, were all evaluated and the findings incorporated in the reviewed licence if granted. Herbal products with medicinal claims were included in the 39,000 PLRs.

A specialist sub-committee on Herbal Standards was set up to advise the S4 Committees. This sub-committee set minimum specifications for large numbers of herbal materials that were on the market.

After three years it was found that the *therapeutic category* approach was rather slow and cumbersome. This was because frequent consultations with the licence holders, amendments to recommendations, and appeals to the CRM and the Medicines Commission consumed a lot of valuable time. In the three years only one category per year had been covered.

In 1979 a second phase of review began where individual products were considered at an early stage without prior consultation with the licence holder. The rate of review increased. It was during this phase that the painkiller phenacetin was banned because of its toxic effects on the kidneys and blood in long-term administration. Bromides, used for their sedative and anti-convulsant properties, were also banned, again because of a variety of toxic effects after prolonged administration. During this time the CRM made recommendations on the appropriate use of barbiturates and benzodiazepines, medicines used in the management of anxiety, sleeplessness and neurosis. However, further recommendations were abandoned as this open policy provoked a lot of controversy and led to difficulties in the review of licences.

An *accelerated procedure* was initiated in this second phase to ensure that those products which gave rise to safety concerns were given priority. To facilitate this procedure, those products remaining to be reviewed were classified into groups where those with possible problems with safety and efficacy were given priority assessment and brought to the CRM as early as possible. This accelerated procedure threw up hazards such as those associated with the taking of medicines containing the elements antimony, arsenic, bismuth, boron, lead and tin, and the administration of the anti-bacterial neomycin by aerosol which had caused deafness in children.

Reviewed licences were still not being processed fast enough to meet the EC deadline of May 1990 and so a third and final phase was entered whereby prescription only medicines (POMs) were dealt with first, followed by over-the-counter (OTC), that is non-prescription, medicines. A more pragmatic approach was adopted in dealing with those medicines for minor self-limiting ailments. Negotiations with licence holders resulted in the removal of unsubstantiated medicinal claims and unnecessary ingredients in the formulations.

The review of those products on the UK market in 1971 and those whose licences were granted between 1971 and 1976 (when EC Directive 75/318/EEC took effect) - a further 1300 - was completed only one year behind the scheduled date of May 1990. During this time just under 5,300 reviewed licences had been granted. All the others, through the activity of the LA with advice from the CRM, had either been allowed to lapse by the licence holders or been revoked by the LA.

Products excluded from the 1990 deadline by EC Directive 75/318/EEC, that is blood products, immunologicals and radiopharmaceuticals, were brought under the control of the Pharmaceutical Directives by the 'Extension Directives', which applied to new applications from January 1992 and to existing products, including those with full UK licences, from 31 December 1992.
A Homoeopathic Directive will take effect from December 1993, when a special registration scheme requiring proof of safety and quality will cover homoeopathic products for oral or topical use which make no claims. Others will be eligible for consideration under the normal EC rules for licensing or, if a member state so decides, under special national rules for marketing only in that member state.

Review, of course, is an on-going process and all products are *reviewed* when their licences are due for renewal every five years or when a new pattern of adverse effects emerges from prolonged patient use.

THE EUROPEAN COMMUNITY

The European Economic Community (EEC), now generally referred to as the EC, was established by a treaty signed in Rome on 25 March 1957, by Belgium, France, the then Federal Republic of Germany, Italy, Luxembourg and the Netherlands. The UK joined, with Denmark and Ireland, in 1973. Greece joined in 1979; Portugal and Spain in 1986.

The population of the twelve Member States is about 337 million, which includes the 17 million of the former German Democratic Republic now integrated with the Federal Republic of Germany.

It is the aim of the EC to have a *single* market in pharmaceuticals among Member States. Until now the different national regulatory requirements of each Member State and the lack of *mutual recognition* of each member's marketing authorisations (equivalent to UK product licences) presented barriers to an internal market in medicinal products.

The Community set up a number of institutions to carry out its aims. The European Commission is the policy making body. It controls a number of Directorates-General (DG's).

Unit C2 of DG III is responsible for:

- preparing proposals for the legislation controlling human and veterinary medicinal products;

- the Committee for Proprietary Medicinal Products (CPMP);

- the Committee for Veterinary Medicinal Products (CVMP);

- the Pharmaceutical Committee.

- **Legislation**

EC legislation is built round a core of key Directives (65/65/EEC;75/318/EEC and 75/319/EEC) all amended and extended by later Directives. These set out the criteria for meeting the requirements of safety, quality and efficacy before *marketing authorisation* is granted. The Directives also lay down procedures for the harmonising of applications, expert reports and the summary of product characteristics (SPC, similar to UK Data Sheets). Aspects of manufacture, wholesale dealing and the dissemination of information are included in Directive requirements.

- **Human Medicines**

Directive 75/319/EEC set up the CPMP which meets regularly in Brussels.

The current role of the CPMP is to:

- give non-binding opinions on applications for marketing authorisation of human medicines made under the Concertation procedure and to review objections raised by Member States under the Multi-state procedure (see below for more details);

- consider matters of Community interest referred to it by a Member State where the grant, suspension or revocation of a marketing authorisation is involved;

- act as a forum for the harmonisation of assessment procedures and the requirements for the testing of all medicinal products in relation to safety, quality and efficacy and to produce agreed guidance on procedures and technical requirements for applications for marketing authorisation;

- establish working parties to assist the CPMP in its work.

Working parties on the following topics have been set up to prepare guidelines and make recommendations to the CPMP:

    Safety
    Pharmacovigilance
    Efficacy
    Quality
    Biotechnology/Pharmacy
    Operations

There is also a working party of the Commission which addresses inspection and manufacturing issues, including the drafting of the Guide to GMP and its annexes.

- **Veterinary Medicines**

The CVMP has a similar role for the consideration of veterinary medicines.

- **The Pharmaceutical Committee**

The Pharmaceutical Committee considers policy matters rather than technical matters and meets as necessary.

- **CPMP Procedures**

- **The Concertation Procedure**

In July 1987 Directive 87/22/EEC was implemented whereby regulatory authorities in the Member States of the EC are required to consult each other (the *Concertation* procedure) before granting, refusing or withdrawing marketing authorisation for medicinal products produced by means of biotechnological processes.

This requirement to consult was introduced to enable the community to pool its scarce resources when considering these new and complex products. It is also intended to lead to uniform decisions throughout the community for products many of which are for specialised and potentially small markets. It also creates the climate for a potentially strong EC biotechnology industry.

In addition to products of biotechnology the Concertation procedure may be used for *high technology* medicinal products (see List B below) provided that the competent authorities and CPMP agree.

Another objective of Directive 87/22/EEC is to confer protection from a second applicant's product coming on the market without the originator's consent until 10 years have elapsed from the date of the first marketing authorisation. The second applicant must then meet the requirements of Article 4.8(a) (amended) of Directive 65/65/EEC.

Directive 87/22/EEC contains 2 separate lists of products:

- List A (Concertation procedure obligatory)

    Products developed by means of recombinant DNA technology; controlled expression of genes coding for biologically active proteins in prokaryotes and eukaryotes, including transformed mammalian cells; and hybridoma and monoclonal antibody methods.

- List B (requested Concertation procedure to be approved)

    Products other than those in List A, which are produced by new methods of technology or other biotechnological processes which constitute significant innovation or which are of significant therapeutic interest.

When using the Concertation procedure applicants must choose whichever Member State they wish to act on their behalf. This Member State is called the Rapporteur. A regulatory control member of staff of this Member State acts as the contact point and co-ordinator for the applicant. When an application intended for the Concertation procedure is received it must be referred to the CPMP.

An applicant may claim exemption from the Concertation procedure for a product that is of interest in one Member State only. In this case assurance has to be given that a similar application has not been made in another Member State within the last 5 years and that within the next 5 years there is no intention to do so. If, however, an application is made within the next 5 years the product must be referred to the CPMP for an opinion.

- **The Multi-State Procedure**

In November 1976 Articles 9 to 11 of Directive 75/319/EEC implemented the *CPMP procedure* whereby an applicant having obtained marketing authorisation in one Member State could apply simultaneously in five or more Member States to obtain similar marketing authorisation. The first Member State was requested to send a copy of the authorisation with relevant documents and particulars as specified in Directive 65/65/EEC (Article 4) to the other nominated Member States.

This first attempt at what may be considered an approach to *mutual recognition* did not prove to be very effective. Only 41 applications were made in eight years and of these 28 received a favourable opinion and 13 did not.

A number of important changes were made to the procedures in Directive 83/570/EEC and implemented in November 1985. The procedure was re-named the *Multi-State procedure* and proved more popular.

The number of applications made in the years which followed were, on average, about 40 per year.

The changes were:

- the minimum number of other Member States was reduced from five to two,

- the facility for having a *Hearing* before the CPMP was introduced,

- In addition to copies of assessment report documentation and marketing authorisation from the first Member State an SPC was included in the package.

European legislation takes precedence over separate national legislation which needs to be amended from time to time to be in line with European requirements. For the foreseeable future there will still be a need for national legislation to implement EC Directives and to deal with products which are intended solely for the domestic market.

The EC Directives have had some success in harmonising medicines licensing arrangements, but have not been able to overcome Member States' reluctance to accept licences issued by other Member States. To overcome this, and so complete the single market in pharmaceuticals, the Commission has proposed new European licensing arrangements, *Future Systems* for short. These will consist of *Centralised* and *Decentralised* control procedures affecting all Member States, supported by a new European Medicines Evaluation Agency (EMEA), whose location should be decided by the end of 1993. In contrast to the non-binding opinion of the CPMP the decisions of the European Commission will be mandatory and binding on all Member States.

It is proposed that the *Centralised Procedure* (replacing the Concertation Procedure) dealing with certain categories of active substances will begin on 1 January 1995 along with the *Decentralised Procedure* (replacing the Multi-state Procedure) which will be optional to applicants for marketing authorisation for the next three years, becoming mandatory in 1998.

Figures 5 and 6 outline the legal framework in the EC and the future systems.

FIGURE 5

MEDICINES REGULATION IN THE EC
THE LEGAL FRAMEWORK

DIRECTIVE 75/318	DIRECTIVE 65/65	DIRECTIVE 75/319
Sets out data requirements for testing	The 'first' directive: sets out the regulatory ground rules	Sets up multi-state procedure and CPMP

EXTENDED BY:

NEW PRODUCTS

DIRECTIVE 89/342
Immunologicals

DIRECTIVE 89/343
Radiopharmaceuticals

DIRECTIVE 89/381
Blood products

DIRECTIVE 92/73
Homeopathics

NEW REQUIREMENTS

DIRECTIVE 91/356
Principles and guidelines of good manufacturing practice

DIRECTIVE 91/507
Updates ANNEX 75/318

DIRECTIVE 92/25
Wholesale distribution

DIRECTIVE 92/26
Legal status

DIRECTIVE 92/27
Labels and leaflets

DIRECTIVE 92/28
Advertising

NEW PROCEDURES

DIRECTIVE 87/22
Sets up concertation procedure

PROPOSED FUTURE SYSTEMS

1 REGULATION,
3 DIRECTIVES

Centralised licensing procedure

Decentralised licensing procedure

European Medicines Evaluation Agency (EMEA)

FIGURE 6

FUTURE MEDICINES LICENSING SYSTEMS

COMPLETING THE SINGLE MARKET IN PHARMACEUTICALS

TIMETABLE FOR IMPLEMENTATION

- 1995: Centralised procedure starts to operate
- 1995 - 1998: Decentralised procedure optional
- 1998: Decentralised procedure obligatory for applications in more than one member state

LEGISLATION

- 1 COUNCIL REGULATION
- 3 COUNCIL DIRECTIVES

KEY FEATURES

- CENTRALISED LICENSING PROCEDURE FOR CERTAIN HIGH-TECHNOLOGY PRODUCTS
- INDUSTRY NOMINATION OF RAPPORTEURS
- DECENTRALISED LICENSING PROCEDURE FOR OTHER PRODUCTS
- EUROPEAN MEDICINES EVALUATION AGENCY

PART THREE

Safety
Patient Information
Advertising

PHARMACOVIGILANCE BUSINESS

THE KEY FUNCTIONS

POST MARKETING DRUG EVALUATION

INFORMATION PROVISION

PATIENT INFORMATION LEAFLETS

ACTION FOR DRUG SAFETY

REGULATION OF MEDICINES PROMOTION

INTERNATIONAL CO-OPERATION

EUROPEAN LIAISON

REGULATORY ACTION

KEEPING A VIGILANT EYE ON WHAT HAPPENS AFTER MARKETING

Before a product is marketed, experience of its safety and efficacy is limited to its use in clinical trials. The conditions under which patients are studied pre-marketing do not necessarily reflect the way the medicine will be used in hospital or in general practice once it is marketed. No matter how extensive the pre-clinical work in animals, and the clinical trials in patients, certain adverse effects may not be detected until a very large number of people have received the medicine. Clinical trials in patients extend, at the most, to only several thousand patients whereas, when marketed, a product may be taken by millions. All medicines are therefore monitored carefully once they are on the market in order to collect information on their side-effects when used in every-day practice. This information may identify unexpected side-effects or indicate that certain side-effects occur more commonly than previously believed, or that some patients are more susceptible to some problems than others. Such findings can lead to changes in the product licence, for example, refinement of dose instructions or the introduction of specific warnings of side-effects, which allow medicines to be used more safely and effectively.

• Monitoring adverse reactions

The LA attaches great importance to the monitoring of possible adverse reactions to medicinal products and uses a variety of methods for collecting such information. Doctors, dentists and coroners are encouraged to report suspected adverse drug reactions and there is a legal requirement for companies to report suspected adverse reactions to their products to the LA. A register of suspected adverse reactions is maintained, which consists of confidential reports about individual patients made on specially designed pre-paid *yellow cards* which are issued to all doctors and dentists. These provide early warnings of potential drug hazards. Summaries of information stored in the register are available to those who report suspected adverse reactions. The identities of patients and reporting doctors from these reports are never disclosed.

A new computer system called Adverse Drug Reactions On-line Information Tracking (ADROIT) was introduced in 1991 to support the monitoring of suspected adverse drug reactions in the UK. This system makes use of information technology, including image processing, to improve the speed and effectiveness of monitoring suspected adverse drug reactions.

In addition to monitoring reports of suspected adverse reactions, post-marketing surveillance studies are conducted by pharmaceutical companies. These studies are performed for the purpose of assessing the safety of medicines in normal usage and further evaluating possible safety concerns.

A variety of studies, of importance in evaluating the short, and long-term effects of medicines, are also conducted by independent researchers throughout the world and these are regularly reviewed by the LA. There is close collaboration between the UK, LA and other drug regulatory authorities both within and outside the EC regarding the monitoring of suspected adverse reactions. The UK is a member of the WHO's Collaborating Centre for International Drug Monitoring, whereby suspected adverse reaction reports are shared with over 30 other countries.

Information from all these sources is carefully screened to identify new side effects and changing patterns of known side effects. The LA acts promptly to ensure that product licences reflect any new information, and advice to doctors, pharmacists and patients is kept up to date to ensure the safe use of medicines.

Rarely, major safety hazards are identified which require severe restriction in the way a medicine is used. If the hazard is considered unacceptable, a medicine may have to be withdrawn from the market. There are powers under the Medicines Act to vary, revoke or suspend product licences under such circumstances. Advice is sought from the advisory bodies of the LA on these matters and companies have rights of appeal against licensing action except in the case of suspension of a licence, when immediate action is taken by the LA.

- **Communication with the health care professions**

Communication with the health care professions, both to warn about adverse effects and to provide feedback of information, is an important aspect of monitoring adverse reactions.

Doctors and pharmacists receive a bulletin called *Current Problems* which alerts them to various problems with medicines and provides advice on the ways medicines may be used more safely. For urgent warnings about drug hazards, letters are sent to all doctors and pharmacists by the CSM. A doctor or dentist who submits a suspected adverse reaction report is sent a copy of the relevant part of the print-out of the register of adverse reactions. Articles by members of MCA and CSM are published in professional journals.

Figure 7 summarises the above activities.

FIGURE 7

POST MARKETING DRUG EVALUATION

REQUIRES A BROAD-BASED STRATEGY
USING A VARIETY OF METHODS FOR:

- LONG -TERM SURVEILLANCE OF ALL MEDICINES.
- RISK BENEFIT ANALYSIS IN THE CONTEXT OF NEW ADRs
  OR CHANGING ADR PROFILES.
- PERIODIC SYSTEMATIC REVIEW OF MEDICINES TO
  RE-EVALUATE RISKS AND BENEFITS.

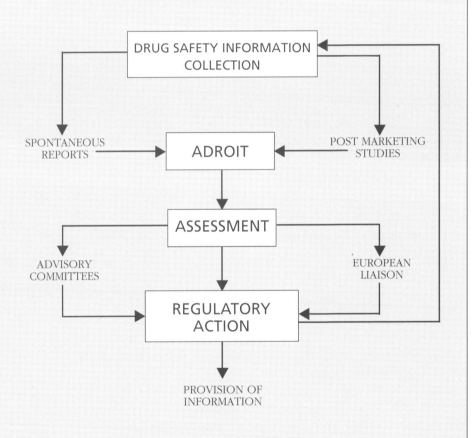

• Inspection

Medicines Inspectors are the MCA's eyes and ears out in the field of pharmaceutical manufacturing. They are based in four regional offices across the country and are in constant touch with headquarters based in London. Manufacturers are inspected to ensure that they comply with the requirements of the product licence as well as demonstrating that manufacturing procedures meet the EC published requirements for GMP. This includes manufacture overseas of products intended for the UK market.

Inspections are carried out regularly and reports submitted for consideration and action by a group at headquarters called the Inspection Action Group (IAG) which comprises lawyers, pharmaceutical and medical assessors, senior inspectors and a range of experts from the MCA, the Department of Health and the MAFF as necessary. When a defective product is reported to the LA the Medicines Inspectorate is involved at every stage of action.

• Defective products

Significant quality defects in products which could present a safety hazard are fortunately very rare and usually relate to individual batches or groups of products, but manufacturers are required to report them to the Defective Medicines Report Centre (DMRC) of the MCA. Reports may also come from users. Following consideration of a defect report, affected batches may need to be recalled. A recall may be needed for example in the case of serious mislabelling, microbial contamination or incorrect ingredients when it is considered that administration of the product would constitute a serious health hazard. Recall is then undertaken by the manufacturer, wholesale dealers, etc, in consultation with the LA. Any country to which the product had been exported is also informed.

• Medicines Testing

The Inspection and Enforcement business contracts testing of raw materials and finished products to outside laboratories, particularly the Medicines Testing Laboratory of the RPSGB in Edinburgh. Approximately 1500 samples are tested each year both to investigate a specific manufacturing deficiency or reported defect and to monitor the quality of a particular product group under investigation. Feedback of the findings goes to the manufacturers concerned and, apart from the occasional need to take rapid action, general improvement in quality is the result.

The Defect Medicines Report Centre is accessible 24 hours every day of the year and handles, on average, 200 reports of suspected quality defects per year. Only about 50 of these will result in recalling a batch of the product from the market. The following are notified urgently of recall by DMRC:

- **Suppliers** of the medicines : Hospitals, Pharmacies, Family Health Service Authorities

- **Health Boards and Health Authorities**

- **Manufacturers and Wholesalers**

- **Ministers, Chief Medical and Chief Pharmaceutical Officers**

- **Other Government Departments**

- **EC Member States** and any other country which has imported the product.

- **Consumers** by means of news media when a defect presents an immediate, serious and widespread hazard. The text of a message is authorised by the Chief Executive of the MCA and passed to the Press Office for onward transmission to Television, Radio and Press.

Follow-up action is then taken by the Medicines Inspectorate, who visit the licence holder/manufacturer to decide on the next course of action.

Figures 8 and 9 outline the Inspection Sequence and the analytical quality control exercised during the life cycle of a medicinal product.

FIGURE 8

INSPECTION SEQUENCE

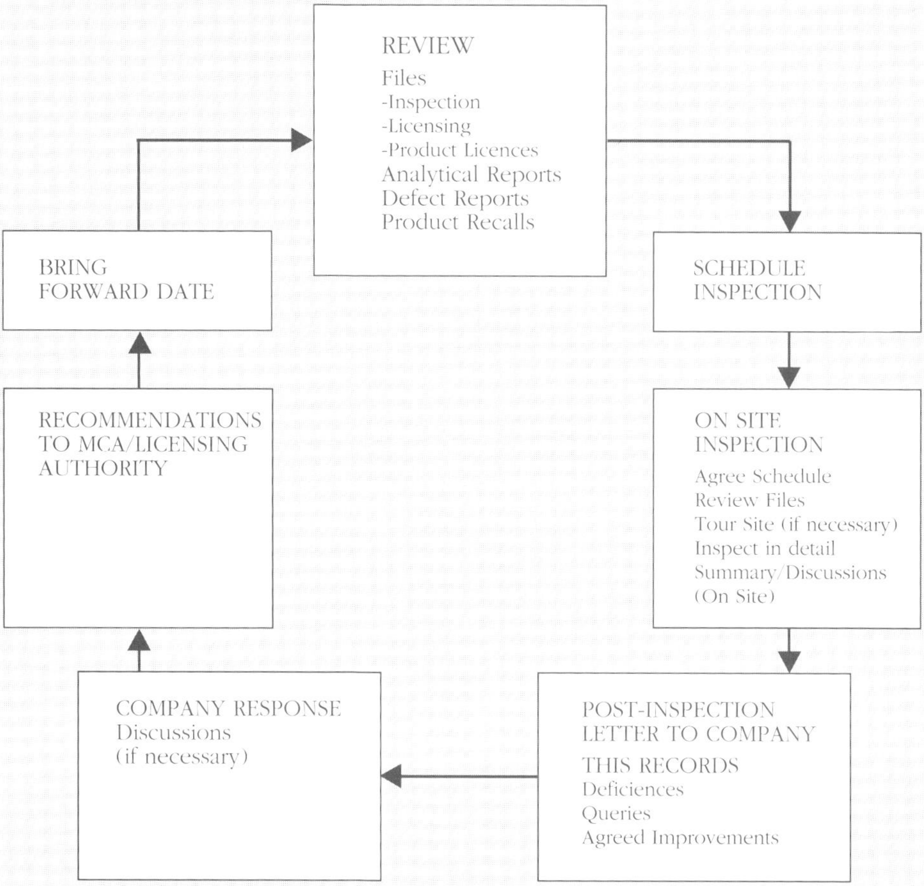

REVIEW

Files
-Inspection
-Licensing
-Product Licences
Analytical Reports
Defect Reports
Product Recalls

SCHEDULE INSPECTION

BRING FORWARD DATE

ON SITE INSPECTION

Agree Schedule
Review Files
Tour Site (if necessary)
Inspect in detail
Summary/Discussions
(On Site)

RECOMMENDATIONS TO MCA/LICENSING AUTHORITY

COMPANY RESPONSE
Discussions
(if necessary)

POST-INSPECTION LETTER TO COMPANY

THIS RECORDS
Deficiences
Queries
Agreed Improvements

INSPECTIONS

Usually result from:

GMP MONITORING REQUIREMENTS
LICENCE APPLICATIONS
LICENCE VARIATIONS
REQUESTS FOR ADVICE

Can result from:

DEFECT REPORTS
ENFORCEMENT ACTION

FIGURE 9

ANALYTICAL QUALITY CONTROL

PRODUCT LIFE CYCLE

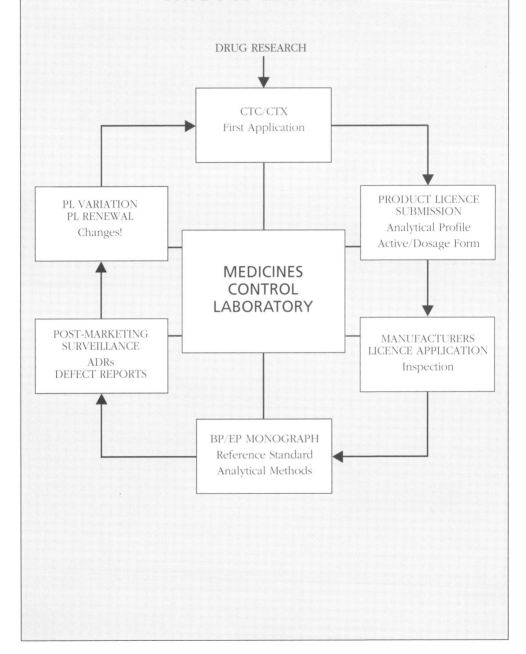

INFORMATION PROVIDED TO PATIENTS ABOUT THEIR MEDICINES

It is very important for patients to read carefully the instructions and warnings on labels before taking their medicines. They should seek advice from their pharmacist or their doctor if they are unsure of these instructions.

Patient Information Leaflets (PILs) give consumers further information about their medicines explaining, for example, how to take the medicine effectively and giving details of warnings along with other information. Presently, there is no obligation for a company to supply a leaflet with a medicine but, if one is supplied, it must be approved by the LA before issue and comply with regulations which set out the information which must be included. An EC Directive (92/27/EEC) was adopted on 31 March 1992 which makes the provision of package leaflets obligatory unless all the required information is on the pack or label. The Directive lists the required information and also lays down the order in which the information should normally be presented in leaflets which will continue to be approved by the LA. New medicines must comply with this Directive from 1 January 1994 and existing medicines will need to comply with this requirement from their next licence renewal after 1 January 1994.

Figure 10 gives the information required to be included on packs and leaflets.

FIGURE 10

EC DIRECTIVE ON LABELS/LEAFLETS
(92/27/EEC)

- TAKES EFFECT 1.1.94
- DETAILS REQUIRED ON PACK OR LEAFLET

• NAME	• ROUTE OF ADMINISTRATION
• ALL INGREDIENTS	• DURATION OF TREATMENT
• FORM	• OVERDOSE ACTION
• TYPE OF ACTIVITY	• IF DOSES MISSED
• PL HOLDER & MANUFACTURER	• WITHDRAWAL EFFECTS
• INDICATIONS	• SIDE EFFECTS
• CONTRA-INDICATIONS	• EXPIRY DATE
• WARNINGS, PRECAUTIONS	• SPECIAL STORAGE INSTRUCTIONS
• INTERACTIONS	• DATE OF LEAFLET
• DOSAGE	

- ANY OTHER INFORMATION TO BE:
  - COMPATIBLE WITH SPC
  - USEFUL FOR HEALTH INFORMATION
  - NON-PROMOTIONAL

ADVERTISING AND PROMOTION OF MEDICINAL PRODUCTS

The term *advertisement* is defined very widely in the Medicines Act and includes virtually any communication which brings the availability of a medicinal product to the attention of the public or of practitioners. It covers newspapers, journals, direct mail advertising, letters, posters, photographs, films and radio and TV broadcasts. Oral representations and Data Sheets are also included under the regulations on promotional activities.

Each licence specifies the recommended use of the product. It is an offence to advertise the product for any other use. Advertisements must not give a false description or be likely to mislead about the nature or quality of the product, its effects or the purposes for which it may or may not be used.

In addition to these general controls there are regulations directed at advertising to the public and at advertising to medical and dental practitioners.

• Advertising to the public

Regulations made under the Act control the advertising to the public of medicinal products and provide that it is an offence to advertise any medicinal product for the treatment of certain diseases such as cancer or sexually transmitted disease. The advertising of medicinal products which are available only on prescription from a doctor or dentist is prohibited. Representations and advertisements in respect of certain specified diseases or conditions which are considered unsuitable for self treatment are also prohibited. These regulations were made to deal primarily with medicines which had been on the market before licensing began and before they had been reviewed. Now that the review is complete the requirements of these regulations are incorporated, as they have always been, in the terms of licences as granted. Generally speaking these regulations restrict advertising to the symptomatic relief of less serious conditions that can be diagnosed by the layperson. Limited exemptions are provided for herbal, homoeopathic and other *traditional medicines.*

• Promotion and advertising to doctors and dentists

If a product is promoted to doctors or dentists a Data Sheet must have been sent or delivered to them within the previous 15 months. A Data Sheet is a document containing basic information about the composition, uses, dosage, side-effects, contra-indications and warnings relating to a medicinal product. The Data Sheet must be consistent with the product licence.

Regulatory controls on advertising to practitioners stipulate that product information, consistent with that provided in the product licence and Data Sheet must appear as part of most written advertisements, for example, those in journals and those addressed personally to doctors or dentists. The information that must be given includes the name and address of the product licence holder and the product licence number; an indication of the active ingredients using non-proprietary (non-branded) names; one or more of the authorised indications for use; side-effects, precautions and contra-indications (summarised); dosage and method of use. The unqualified use of the word *safe* is prohibited, as are misleading graphs and tables.

These regulations for medicinal product licences enable the LA to exercise controls over advertisements for particular products, either by requiring all advertisements to be submitted in advance or by requiring that certain particulars should be included or by requiring that individual advertisements be amended or withdrawn. The ABPI and the PAGB operate Codes of Practice for prescription-only medicines and over-the-counter medicines respectively. This process of self-regulation together with the legal provisions under the Medicines Act and, in future, the EC Directives control all aspects of the promotion of medicines.

An EC Directive (92/28/EEC) was adopted on 31 March 1992 and became effective from 1 January 1993. This provides a common framework for advertising and promotion of medicinal products within the Community. It is similar to existing UK practice and sets out criteria with which all pharmaceutical advertising must comply. It imposes a general prohibition on the advertising of prescription only medicines to the public and confirms the principle that all advertising must reflect the terms of the marketing authorisation and must not be misleading in any way.

Figure 11 sets out action which may be taken on the promotion of medicinal products to the public.

FIGURE 11

ACTION ON MEDICINES PROMOTION

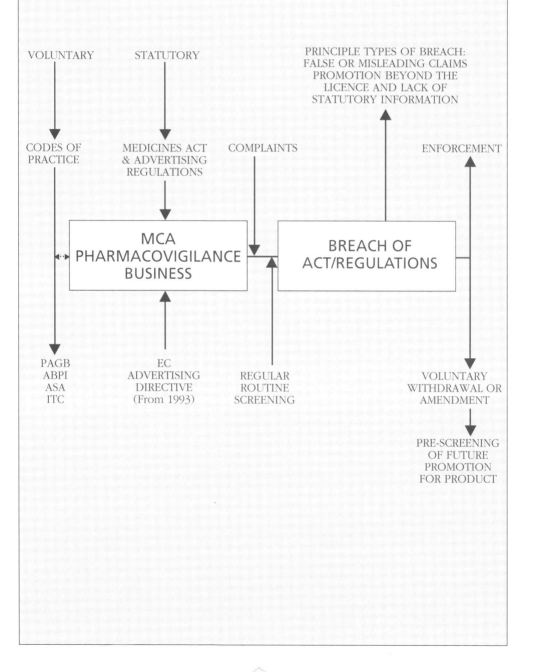

PART FOUR

The United Kingdom
Medicines Control Agency

THE UNITED KINGDOM MEDICINES CONTROL AGENCY

It was mentioned earlier that the Licensing Authority of the UK comprises a body of government health ministers whose executive function in the control of medicines is performed on a day-to-day basis by the UK Medicines Control Agency (MCA). The MCA is an executive agency of the Department of Health and was established in April 1989 following a re-organisation of the former Medicines Division of the Department of Health.

The primary purpose of the MCA is to safeguard public health by ensuring that human medicines available in the UK are made to the highest standards of quality and are evaluated for safety and efficacy before and after they are approved and licensed for sale and supply. The MCA also aims to provide an efficient and cost-effective service that does not impede the pharmaceutical industry's continuing efforts in research and development directed at finding new and better medicines which are in all our interests.

The published policy statement of the MCA is as follows:

The Medicines Control Agency seeks to:

- *serve Ministers with excellence and help implement the Government's objectives for health;*

- *discharge its responsibilities to the public health by ensuring that all medicines on the UK market meet acceptable standards of safety, quality and efficacy;*

- *deliver the highest standards of service consistent with discharging these responsibilities;*

- *match income with expenditure on an accruals basis and break even taking one year with another;*

- *ensure value for money in its procurement and delivery of services;*

- *achieve its objectives without misusing its monopoly position or causing undue impediment to the progress or development of the pharmaceutical industry;*

- *treat all staff fairly and responsibly and offer them a career limited only by ambition, ability and the availability of opportunities within the MCA.*

The MCA is organised into five multi-disciplinary businesses and a Finance Directorate which report to the Chief Executive. Legal advice is provided by the Department of Health Solicitors' office.

Figure 12 gives an outline of the organisation.

FIGURE 12

ORGANISATION:
MCA BOARD OF MANAGEMENT

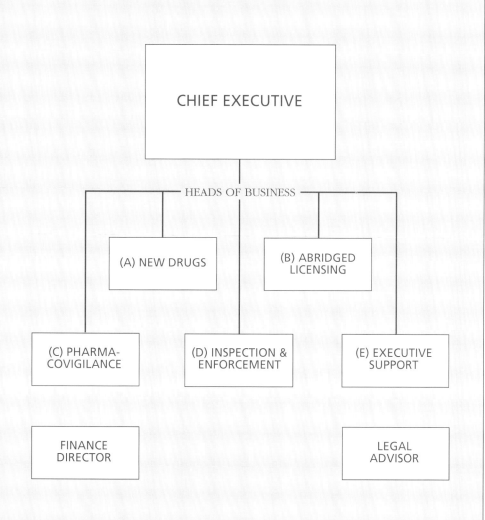

NEW DRUGS BUSINESS

The New Drugs Business is responsible for the licensing of new active substances in the UK. The term *new active substance* means that the active ingredient in a medicine has not previously been licensed for use in the UK in any dosage form. This covers both new chemical materials and materials of biological and biotechnological origin. The development of a new medicinal product is a major undertaking for any pharmaceutical company. The process of discovery and development is complicated and expensive, extending over many years. The quantity of data generated and submitted to the LA is substantial. The average amount of data per application submitted in the last few years was 170 volumes, each one the size of a telephone directory.

In the movement towards a *Single European Market* the European Support Group is responsible for negotiating the *future systems* proposals that will apply across the Community and for the activities relating to these negotiations. This Business is responsible for the UK participation in the CPMP licensing work. The UK has taken a major role in this activity with more than 40% of applications being handled by the UK. There has also been considerable input into recent debate and drafting of new Directives affecting medicinal products.

A third main area of activity concerns the initial assessment and the subsequent supervision of all clinical trials undertaken on patients in the UK. These give important clues to the types of new medicinal products which are likely to come on to the market in the years following the completion of successful trials.

The Business is also responsible for the preparation of the BP, a publicly-available collection of specifications for the quality of medicines; for organising and co-ordinating the UK's involvement in the Ph Eur; and for devising British Approved Names (BAN's) for medicinal substances. Compliance with pharmacopoeial standards is usually shown by the letters *BP* or *Ph Eur* after a name on a label. This is a recognition of the hallmark of quality demanded by the LA and contributes to consumer confidence in the product.

The Business is divided into the following main areas of activity as indicated in Figure 13.

FIGURE 13

NEW DRUGS

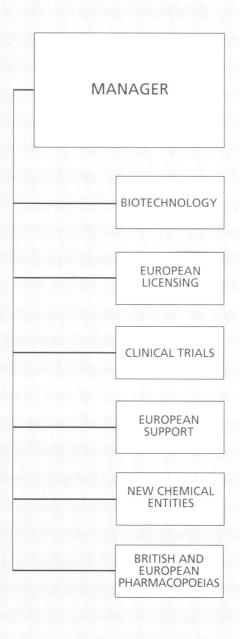

ABRIDGED LICENSING BUSINESS

The Abridged Licensing Business is responsible for the initial processing of all product licence applications and applications to vary product licences in the UK and for issuing licences for all UK products. In addition, it undertakes the scientific assessment of all product licence applications and variations except those for new active substances, biotechnological and most biological products. New active substances falling into the Dental, Surgical and Radiopharmaceutical fields, however, are assessed by this Business. The review of medicinal products already on the market when the Medicines Act became law (see Part Two) was concluded by this Business.

Abridged licence applications are so described because the active constituents of medicinal products are not new products but materials which have already been licensed in similar or other pharmaceutical forms and where the clinical profile has been largely established. The data requirements, therefore, are generally less than those for new active substances. Examples include new strengths of existing products, new formulations such as controlled release, new indications for established drugs and generic versions of proprietary medicines.

As mentioned in Part One, product licences are granted for up to five years and these must be renewed if companies wish to continue marketing the products beyond that time. The Abridged Licensing Business deals with this aspect of licensing as well as variations to licences during their five-year life. Because of the continuous progress and updating of manufacturing and packaging procedures and the watchful activity of the Pharmacovigilance Business, requests for variations occupy a substantial part of this Business's activity. Around ten thousand applications to vary licences are dealt with each year.

Some CPMP multi-state applications are dealt with by this business which is also involved in EC proposals affecting general licensing issues, for example, it is leading negotiations for the UK in the proposed new EC rules for variations. The Business is responsible for licensing policy on complementary medicines and represented the UK in negotiating the EC Homoeopathic Directive. It also liaises with the Department of Health and Medical Devices Directorate in deciding the future European safety controls for devices such as drug infusion pumps. The Abridged Licensing Business provides the UK input to the EC voluntary work-sharing exercise on Radiopharmaceuticals under the EC Extension Directives as well as supplying the administrative support to the Task Force working on all products covered by the Extension Directives.

Medicinal products which have marketing authorisations in any Member State of the EC may be imported into the UK for marketing under a parallel import scheme, provided that there is a related UK licence. These licence applications are assessed by professional staff to determine whether, the product to be imported into the U.K. is theraputically equivalent to the one already licensed in the U.K. and that the labelling is in English and in accordance with UK legal requirements.

Figure 14 summarises area of responsibility.

FIGURE 14

ABRIDGED LICENSING

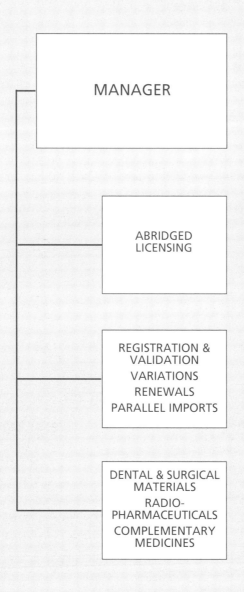

PHARMACOVIGILANCE BUSINESS

From the moment a new medicinal product is marketed a watchful eye is kept on the pattern of adverse effects that may emerge from its administration to larger numbers of patients. The Pharmacovigilance Business is responsible for this aspect of the MCA's activity. It is particularly concerned that the safety of medicinal products, as described in the data presented to support an application for a product licence, is confirmed during use in clinical practice. Newly introduced medicines are kept under intensive surveillance for at least two years. Information from many different sources is used to monitor continuously the risks and benefits of all medicines and make changes to the ways medicines are used to improve their safety. As new information emerges on the risks and benefits of medicines during widespread clinical use, changes may need to be made to the product licence and to the advice to doctors, pharmacists and patients. These may involve changes to the indications, dose instructions, warnings, contra-indications or the information on side effects. These changes are made by variations to the licence which are then reflected in the data sheet, labelling and patient information leaflets (PILs).

Rarely, very major safety hazards may be identified which indicate that the hazards of the medicine outweigh its benefits. In such circumstances, action is taken to withdraw the medicine from the market by revocation or suspension of the licence. The medical and allied professions are kept informed of important drug safety issues by means of *Current Problems* bulletins and, in the case of a major safety concern, by letters from the Chairman of the CSM.

The Business plays a major international role in drug safety through the WHO Collaborating Centre, the Council for International Organisations of Medical Sciences (CIOMS) Working Groups, and the Pharmacovigilance Working Party of the CPMP. It has taken an important lead in harmonising the approach to drug safety monitoring and assessment both in the EC and world-wide. The Pharmacovigilance Business is also responsible for ensuring that PILs, labelling and advertising meet high standards.

The Business is divided into three areas as indicated in Figure 15.

The Adverse Drug Reactions On-line Information Tracking Unit (ADROIT) is responsible for handling reports on suspected adverse reactions received from doctors, dentists and licence holders. A new computer, introduced in 1991, improved the speed and effectiveness of dealing with all suspected adverse reaction reports.

The Post-Marketing Drug Evaluation Unit is responsible for assessing the risks and benefits of medicines throughout their marketing lives to ensure product information reflects changing experience. Doctors, dentists and pharmacists are kept informed of important safety issues.

The Unit for the control of labelling, patient information and the promotion of medicines monitors and takes appropriate action to maintain high standards in these areas. It is also responsible for implementing EC Directives relating to these matters.

FIGURE 15

PHARMACOVIGILANCE

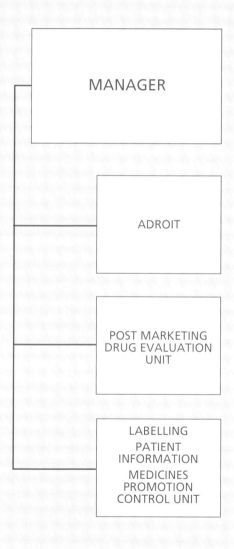

MANAGER

ADROIT

POST MARKETING
DRUG EVALUATION
UNIT

LABELLING

PATIENT
INFORMATION

MEDICINES
PROMOTION
CONTROL UNIT

INSPECTION AND ENFORCEMENT BUSINESS

This Business exists to ensure that medicinal products which have a valid product licence are made and distributed in accordance with EC GMP and in such a way that they comply with the quality standards defined in the licence. Every UK manufacturer and wholesaler of medicinal products is required to have a licence to operate legally. There are nearly 500 manufacturing sites in the UK, each of which is inspected at least every two years. Overseas manufacturers of medicinal products intended to be marketed in the UK are inspected either by the UK Medicines Inspectorate or, on their behalf, by the inspectors in the country where manufacture takes place. The provisions of the Medicines Act are enforced as necessary and many successful prosecutions have been undertaken. Reports of breaches of requirements of the Medicines Act may be received from many sources - health professionals, members of the public, the pharmaceutical industry and other law enforcement authorities.

Variations to a product licence, where a manufacturing process needs to be changed, and variations where a new site of manufacture is involved, need to be approved by both assessors and inspectors before the variation can take place. Where a completely new manufacturing process is to be implemented, or where a new type of dosage form has to be manufactured, an inspection must take place before approval.

A Defective Medicines Report Centre is accessible 24 hours every day of the year and handles, on average, 200 reports per year. (see Part Three, Medicines Testing, for details)

The Inspection and Enforcement Business is responsible for the work of the MCA laboratory at Canons Park in London and for work contracted out on the MCA's behalf to the Royal Pharmaceutical Society's Medicines Testing Laboratory in Edinburgh. Proposed procedures for standard pharmacopoeial monographs are assessed, and methods selected for analytical analysis are checked, as suitable for their intended purpose and capability of reproduction by an independent laboratory. Under a quality monitoring system samples of medicines are selected from production batches for analysis at the Medicines Testing Laboratory in Edinburgh. On average 1500 samples are tested each year.

A further important activity of this Business is the issuing on request of Export Certificates which verify that a product has been made by a licensed manufacturer to EC GMP standards and is regularly inspected. If the product has a PL this will also be stated. The certificate then conforms to the WHO certification scheme. Around 7,000 certificates are issued each year.

Internationally the UK LA is a founder member of the International Pharmaceutical Inspection Convention (PIC). The purpose of the PIC is for members to exchange inspection reports based on common standards of inspection and GMP. This reduces the need for members to do inspections in each others' countries and helps to reinforce common international standards which are of benefit to industry as a whole. In the last few years the UK Medicines Inspectorate has contributed significantly to the dissemination and harmonisation of GMP guidelines, first through the PIC and the EC and more recently as a major contributor to the proposed revision of the WHO guidelines on GMP.

Figure 16 outlines areas of responsibility.

FIGURE 16

INSPECTION AND ENFORCEMENT

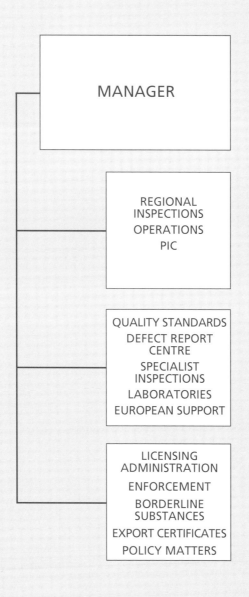

MANAGER

REGIONAL INSPECTIONS
OPERATIONS
PIC

QUALITY STANDARDS
DEFECT REPORT CENTRE
SPECIALIST INSPECTIONS
LABORATORIES
EUROPEAN SUPPORT

LICENSING ADMINISTRATION
ENFORCEMENT
BORDERLINE SUBSTANCES
EXPORT CERTIFICATES
POLICY MATTERS

EXECUTIVE SUPPORT BUSINESS

The Executive Support business was established as a direct result of the re-organisation and restructuring of the former Medicines Division of the Department of Health into the MCA. The aim is to ensure that the other Businesses in the MCA have at their disposal the infrastructure and support they need to perform their work effectively and efficiently. Its role is both to rationalise support services and to develop MCA policies which affect all Businesses. (See Figure 17.)

The primary advisory body to the Licensing Authority (LA), the Medicines Commission (MC), is provided with secretarial and professional support from this Business.

The MCA's Information Technology Services Unit (IT) is managed by the Executive Support Business and plays a key role notably in maintaining all the activities of the various Businesses in the MCA and also in supporting new IT activities.

The Fees Policy Unit is responsible for the development and continuing review of the MCA's licensing fee system implemented in July 1991.

Crucial to the function of any medicines control procedure is a good product licence data base and adequate means of gathering and disseminating the information to those needing it. The Business has integrated these information sources into one comprehensive unit. Library and other information facilities are constantly updated and news of them circulated to staff by means of information sheets. MAIL, a regular update of MCA developments, is sent to all licence holders and others. Figure 18 outlines the activities of the MCA Information Centre.

Other major areas of this Business's activities include the classification of medicines, the custodianship of the Medicines Act and its inter-relationship with European Directives, personnel management, communications and corporate planning. Other Businesses take the lead in scientific and technical areas but the Executive Support Business co-ordinates these activities with the activity of the MCA as a whole. When visitors from both home and overseas wish to know more about the MCA's activity, the Executive Support Business is the point of contact.

FIGURE 17

EXECUTIVE SUPPORT

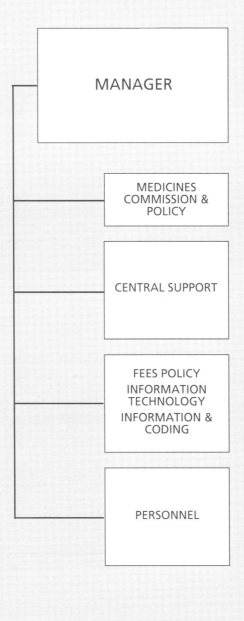

FIGURE 18

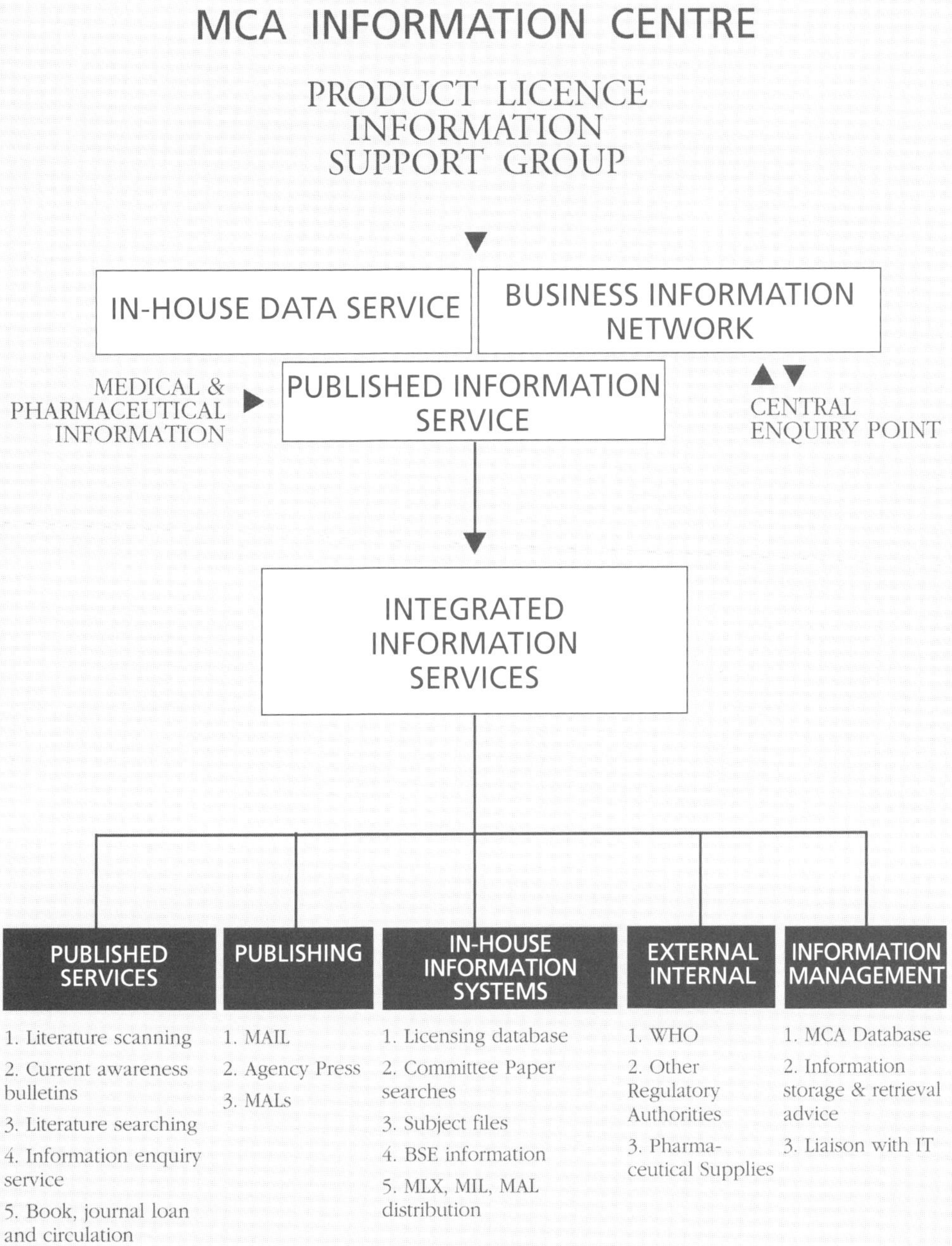

MCA INFORMATION CENTRE

PRODUCT LICENCE
INFORMATION
SUPPORT GROUP

▼

IN-HOUSE DATA SERVICE	BUSINESS INFORMATION NETWORK

MEDICAL &
PHARMACEUTICAL ▶ PUBLISHED INFORMATION
INFORMATION SERVICE

▲▼
CENTRAL
ENQUIRY POINT

▼

INTEGRATED
INFORMATION
SERVICES

PUBLISHED SERVICES	PUBLISHING	IN-HOUSE INFORMATION SYSTEMS	EXTERNAL INTERNAL	INFORMATION MANAGEMENT
1. Literature scanning	1. MAIL	1. Licensing database	1. WHO	1. MCA Database
2. Current awareness bulletins	2. Agency Press	2. Committee Paper searches	2. Other Regulatory Authorities	2. Information storage & retrieval advice
3. Literature searching	3. MALs	3. Subject files	3. Pharma-ceutical Supplies	3. Liaison with IT
4. Information enquiry service		4. BSE information		
5. Book, journal loan and circulation		5. MLX, MIL, MAL distribution		

PART FIVE

Some questions and
answers

SOME QUESTIONS AND ANSWERS

QUESTION: Are there any completely safe medicines?

ANSWER:

A completely safe medicine will probably never exist. Even aspirin can occasionally cause problems; safety is a relative term. When the LA decides whether or not to grant a licence for a medicinal product it balances the risk from possible side-effects against the likely benefit to patients, having had advice from its advisory bodies as necessary. Therefore, a greater risk for perceived benefit may be taken for one product as against another. However, all medicines that are effective have some side-effects and should be used only when needed. The same medicinal product may affect different people in different ways. Medicines are classified into three categories in the UK, that is:

- Prescription Only Medicine (POM) - medicines that can only be dispensed by a pharmacist in a registered pharmacy in accordance with a doctor'sprescription;

- Pharmacy (P) - medicines that can only be sold in a pharmacy under the supervision of a pharmacist;

- General Sale List (GSL) - medicines that may be sold in other outlets, such as supermarkets.

This indicates that some medicines are considered to be appropriate for the public to use without the supervision or advice of a doctor or pharmacist.

QUESTION: Could there ever be another *thalidomide* type disaster?

ANSWER:

Although no absolute guarantee can be given, the chances of this happening again are very remote. This is because of the measures now taken by regulatory authorities to test all new formulations of active substances before they are allowed on to the market and to monitor for unexpected and unacceptable side-effects once marketed. However, a categorical *No* cannot be given to this question since we cannot be sure that such a thing would never happen again.

QUESTION: Are all medicines subjected to clinical trials before coming on to the market?

ANSWER:

All new active substances are subjected to clinical trials. Some established medicines are also subjected to clinical trials, for example, where it is wished to claim a new clinical use for the product.

QUESTION: Are healthy volunteer studies necessary and if so why are they not controlled by legislation, especially when people taking part in such studies have suffered serious side-effects?

ANSWER:

It is not a legal requirement to control healthy volunteer studies. Healthy volunteer studies are part of the normal process of drug development to see what effect a substance has on a healthy person before it is tried in patients. Control of healthy volunteer studies takes the form of regulation by the medical profession through independent ethics committees, which include members other than those in the medical profession. These follow guidelines laid down by the Royal College of Physicians (RCP) and those of the ABPI, covering details in the conduct of the trials, necessary facilities that must be available and the need to have approval of independent ethics committees. The Medicines Commission has also advised the Health Minister on healthy volunteer studies and considers that on presently available information there is no need to bring healthy volunteer studies under statutory control.

QUESTION: What is the difference between *active* and *other* constituents?

ANSWER:

All the constituents that make up a medicine are divided into active and non-active (or other) constituents. As the name suggests, active constituents are those that give the medicine the effects that it is taken for (for example pain relief). Other constituents (for example colours, flavours, sweetening agents, fillers) are there to make the active constituent into a medicine that can be taken by the patient.

QUESTION: What do the letters *BP, Ph Eur* and *USP* after an
ingredient on a label mean?

ANSWER:

The letters mean *British Pharmacopoeia*, *Pharmacopée Européenne* (European
Pharmacopoeia) and *United States Pharmacopoeia* respectively. They indicate
that the ingredients meet a specified minimum standard of quality defined in
that publicly available reference work. However, even if the letters do not
appear after an ingredient but the ingredient name is the same as the name in
the pharmacopoeia it must meet the same standard. For example: *Paracetamol*
and *Paracetamol BP* must comply with the same published standard.

QUESTION: Many constituents listed on the label do not have BP, Ph
Eur or USP after their name. Does this mean that they
are not as safe as those that do?

ANSWER:

All constituents that are used in a medicine that has been licensed in the UK
have been carefully examined and deemed to be safe for the purpose for which
they are being used. Some constituents, such as new active constituents, have
not been licensed long enough for an entry in a Pharmacopoeia to have been
developed.

QUESTION: What is an E-number?

ANSWER:

The E-number is a shorthand way of identifying some substances, such as
colours, which have long and complex names. All constituents of medicines
that are identified by an E-number have been approved in the EC as well as in
the UK.

QUESTION: How is the legal or marketing status of a medicine
changed?

ANSWER:

As indicated in the first question the legal status of a medicine on the UK
market can be POM, P, or GSL. Under the Medicines Act medicinal products
have a P status unless made POM or GSL by listing them in a Statutory
Instrument; either the POM Order or the GSL Order. The first licence for a
medicinal product containing a new active substance is normally given
temporary POM status until such time as the POM Order is updated (about

once a year). Most such products are made POM in this way. Temporary GSL status can be given for two years through a licence or for one year through a variation again until the GSL order is updated. In both cases POM and GSL will revert to P unless the appropriate Order is amended in time. Consultation with interested parties takes place before amendments are made. Safety is the over-riding factor in any move from POM to P or P to GSL. Examples of changes from POM to P status are certain topical hydrocortisone products, ibuprofen, a pain killer, with restricted dose and indications, and imidazoles for vaginal candidiasis. An EC Directive (92/26/EEC) on legal classification was adopted on 31 March 1992 and became effective on 1 January 1993. This sets out the criteria for restricting products to prescription control and provides for review of the legal classification of a product on renewal of its licence, or when new evidence is presented.

QUESTION: How do I know if a medicine has been licensed?

ANSWER:

Somewhere on the label a unique licence number must be stated. For example, PL/1234/5678. The first set of numbers indicates who is the licence holder and the second set the number of that licence holder's particular product.

QUESTION: How often are manufacturers inspected to see if they comply with GMP requirements?

ANSWER:

All manufacturers are inspected initially and must be found to be satisfactory before a manufacturing licence is granted.

There are nearly 500 manufacturing sites in the UK, each of which is inspected thereafter at least every two years. If, however, on inspection certain aspects need urgent attention or a major change is introduced, a follow-up inspection will take place within a much shorter time. Overseas manufacturing sites are inspected in a similar way, either by UK inspectors or by the inspectors of the particular country on behalf of the UK under special arrangements such as the PIC.

QUESTION: How often are wholesale dealers inspected?

ANSWER:

Wholesale dealers are inspected within a maximum time period of 5 years. Importers are inspected within a 2 year period.

QUESTION: What happens if a licence holder changes some aspect of a medicine after it has been approved by the LA?

ANSWER:

A licence holder is legally bound to market a medicinal product in strict accordance with the provisions of the product licence. Before any change is made to these provisions the holder must apply to vary the licence and have the request approved before a change is made. If this is not done the licence holder can be prosecuted and the product removed from the market.

QUESTION: What are generic medicines and are they as good as branded ones?

ANSWER:

When a new active substance is first marketed the applicant can seek protection to market the product exclusively by means of taking out *patent protection* for a limited number of years. This is to help recover the massive research and development costs of finding and marketing the new product. The product is normally given a proprietary or branded name. When patent protection expires anyone is free to copy the product and market it using the name of the active constituent. This name is the *generic* name (some generics, however, are given new proprietary names). To be licensed, applications for generic products must be supported by scientific data or studies reported in scientific literature showing that they are *bioequivalent*, that is give the same desired clinical effect, as the original and are, therefore, as good as the branded product.

QUESTION: What are UK parallel imported medicines?

ANSWER:

These are medicines which are:

    marketed in one or more EC Member States as well as in the UK;

    made by the same manufacturer (or under licence, that is by special agreement);

    imported and marketed in the UK by a person other than the manufacturer;

    essentially the same and shown to be bioequivalent, that is have the same clinical effect;

    labelled in English.

The exercise of parallel importing will probably cease when a truly EC single market is achieved.

QUESTION: Is the quality of a medicine the same whether it is manufactured in the UK or overseas?

ANSWER:

Within the EC all manufacturers must be inspected and authorised by National Authorities to the EC standards of GMP.

All importers into the EC must ensure that their sources of supply in countries outside the EC are also appropriately authorised and comply at least with the EC requirements for GMP. For those countries within the PIC inspection reports are mutually exchanged. For other countries an inspection of the manufacturing site may be conducted before a product licence is granted. Surveillance of manufacturing sites in countries outside the EC is continued throughout the life of the product licence.

QUESTION: How quickly does the LA act when it receives reports of adverse drug reactions?

ANSWER:

The MCA receives reports of suspected adverse drug reactions every day from doctors through the UK's spontaneous ADR reporting scheme. Many of these are well-known and are included in the product information. All information on the safety of medicines is carefully screened to identify previously unknown problems or problems that may require change in the way a medicine is used.

A number of factors have to be taken into account before any LA action is taken. For example, how many reports there are for a particular adverse effect and what is the likelihood that these were caused by a particular drug? Was the correct dosage being given? What other medicines was the patient taking? What was the general condition of the patient? Do reports refer to one particular batch of material? Have there been similar reports in other countries? Are the reports serious enough to take drastic action, that is suspend or revoke the licence or would a modification in dosage and indications, with appropriate warnings on the Data Sheet, be sufficient? If a major safety hazard is identified, a medicine can be withdrawn from use immediately.

QUESTION: Are radiopharmaceutical medicines radioactive and `
hence dangerous?

ANSWER:

Radiopharmaceutical medicines contain tiny amounts of radioactive components. They are not dangerous when handled properly and are used mainly for diagnostic or testing purposes although a few are used for the treatment of disease.

QUESTION: Are herbal medicines safe?

ANSWER:

For most of the history of humankind herbs have been the source of medicines. Long established medicines containing such substances as codeine, morphine, digoxin, and atropine are still obtained from plants cultivated commercially across the world. All herbal mixtures making medicinal claims are subject to the same stringent requirements for safety, quality and efficacy as medicines containing purely chemical active ingredients. During the review of those medicinal products on the market when licensing began in 1971 a number of medicines containing herbal ingredients such as Comfrey, Sassafras, Broom, Mistletoe, Berberis and Juniper were evaluated. Some were not considered to be safe and/or effective for their intended use, were not given reviewed licences and have, therefore, ceased to be available in licensed medicinal products. All medicines are subject to post-marketing scrutiny.

QUESTION: What is a homoeopathic medicine?

ANSWER:

A homoeopathic medicine is a medicine containing highly diluted active ingredients prepared by specific homoeopathic manufacturing procedures whose therapeutic value is based on the belief that in a healthy person those ingredients would produce symptoms like the disease being treated.

Homoeopathy emphasises the treatment of the patient rather than the disease so that two patients with the same disease do not necessarily receive the same treatment.

QUESTION: What is a PIL and what is its purpose? Why do some medicines not have them?

ANSWER:

A PIL is a Patient Information Leaflet. It informs patients about their medicine - what kind of medicine it is, with a list of its ingredients; how to take it effectively; what possible side-effects might occur and what to do about them; what foods or liquids to avoid while taking the medicine; and any other special instructions. It has to be written in clear and understandable terms for the patient. From 1 January 1994 all new medicines must have a leaflet unless the required information is on the pack or label. Thereafter all existing medicines will require to have a leaflet by the time their licence comes up for renewal. All leaflets have to be approved in advance by the MCA.

QUESTION: What is a Data Sheet and where can a copy be obtained?

ANSWER:

A Data Sheet is a factual statement about a medicine provided to the medical and dental professions. It is a summary of the main information relating to the medicine - its composition; purpose of uses; correct dosage for different age groups; side-effects, precautions and warnings; storage conditions and shelf-life; the name of the licence holder and the licence number.

Data Sheets are not generally available to the public, most of the necessary information is provided in the label or PIL which is supplied with the medicine. Copies of some Data Sheets can be obtained from most local libraries, by reference to the ABPI Data Sheet Compendium.

QUESTION: What assurance is there that the pharmaceutical industry does not use its position to influence the licensing decisions of the MCA?

ANSWER:

The MCA has a detailed set of staff rules and standard operating procedures to protect the independence of its staff. There are published guidelines covering most areas of scientific interest. The MCA also has a sophisticated system of advisory committees which involves independent experts and advisors to ensure the quality of decisions.

QUESTION: Why is there so much secrecy surrounding the work of the MCA and its advisory bodies?

ANSWER:

The Government is reviewing the requirements of the Medicines Act as part of its *Open Government* policy. Section 118 of the Medicines Act 1968 lays down that information supplied to the LA in connection with the application for, granting, and maintenance of a product licence or clinical trial certificate must be kept in confidence by the LA and its advisory bodies. This is intended to protect the commercial secrets of the pharmaceutical industry. But where there is a safety issue the necessary information is given because the need to protect public health takes priority. Interpretation of this Section of the Act is being kept under review in the light of developments in the EC Single Market to enable more information about the licensing process to be made public.

QUESTION: How long do members of advisory bodies serve on their lrespective committees?

ANSWER:

Members of the Medicines Commission are appointed to serve for four years and can have a second term of service or more. Members of the Section 4 committees and their expert sub-committees are appointed for three years and can also serve a second or even third term of service. Members must declare their interests and where there is a conflict of interest a member must retire from a sitting of the committee until the matter under discussion has been dealt with.

QUESTION: Will the EC take over the licensing of UK medicines?

ANSWER:

The move towards a single European Market involves the setting up of new licensing systems with *centralised* and *decentralised* procedures for the control of medicines (see Part Two). A new European Medicines Evaluation Agency (EMEA) will support this new system. To begin with all new active substances will be handled by the centralised system whereas the decentralised system will involve existing or modified national procedures.

QUESTION: How is the activity of the MCA funded?

ANSWER:

By fees paid by applicants for the granting of licences, variations to licences and inspections of premises and by licence holders for the maintenance of licences once granted.

PART SIX

Conclusion

MCA enquiry point

Department of Health
News Branch and
Press Office

References

CONCLUSION

The concept of mandatory control of medicines requires a satisfactory legal framework within which government administrators and health care professionals can operate and use their skills in the effort to achieve safe, effective medicines. This legal framework is provided by the Medicines Act 1968, its various orders and regulations, and relevant EC Directives from 65/65/EEC onwards. On the three principles of safety, quality and efficacy, an acceptable risk-to-benefit ratio can be reached for each medicinal product.

The UK MCA has about 350 highly qualified and trained staff who work closely with advisory bodies set up under the Medicines Act. The members of these select bodies are eminent practitioners in their respective fields of medicine, pharmacy and related sciences. They give advice to the MCA based upon the most recent scientific findings and professional opinions.

A former chairman of the Committee on Safety of Medicines, Professor Sir Abraham Goldberg, summed up the objectives of medicines regulators when he said:

> *We attempt to steer a middle course between those who believe that drug-regulating authorities suffocate all creative action and thinking in a welter of bureaucracy, and pressure groups and individuals who expect 100 per cent safety from any new drug on the market - an impossible dream. The goal of drug safety is pursued to the limit of contemporary science, and the balanced equation on the control of new drug therapy is always efficacy versus safety. Each judgement is a fine one, based on this most important principle* [3].

[3] Goldberg, A., and Griffin, J. P. Functions of the Committee on Safety of Medicines. UPDATE, London, 1984, Vol 29, No 1, 33

CONTACT POINTS

MCA ENQUIRY POINT

MCA
Central Enquiry Point
Department of Health
Market Towers
1 Nine Elms Lane
Vauxhall
London SW8 5NQ

Tel: 071 273 3000

MCA DEFECTIVE MEDICINES REPORT CENTRE

Accessible 24 hours every day of the year

Tel: 071 273 0574

DEPARTMENT OF HEALTH NEWS BRANCH AND PRESS OFFICE

Department of Health
News Branch and Press Office
Richmond House
79 Whitehall
London SW1A 2NS

Tel: 071 210 5963

REFERENCES

The Medicines Act 1968 and its various Orders and Statutory Instruments.
London: H.M. Stationery Office.

Commission of the European Communities.
The Rules Governing Medicinal Products in the EC.
London: H.M. Stationery Office.

British Pharmacopoeia and its Addenda.
London: HM Stationery Office. _

European Pharmacopoeia.
Sainte-Ruffine, France: Maisonneuve S.A.

Martindale, The Extra Pharmacopoeia.
London: Pharmaceutical Press.

The British National Formulary
Published jointly approximately twice yearly by The BMA and the RPSGB.

Data Sheet Compendium
Published annually by the ABPI.

Technical Information Bulletins
Issued by the Parenteral Drug Association Inc. (USA).

Technical Monographs
Issued by the Parenteral Society of Great Britain.

Monograph Series on GMP
The Institute of Quality Assurance, Pharmaceutical Quality Group (UK).

MAIL - Medicine Act Information Letters.
Issued regularly by the MCA to all licence holders.

Current Problems
Bulletins issued as necessary by the MCA.

Annual Reports
The Medicines Commission, the British Pharmacopoeia Commission, and Section
4 Committees.

The Framework Document of the MCA.

Annual Reports of the MCA.

Printed in the United Kingdom for **HMSO**

Dd. 296436, c50, 10/93 65536 5600 O/No 263159 39/28198